THE BRIDE & GROOM

THANK-YOU

GUIDE

WITHDRAWN
PRINT

THE BRIDE & GROOM
THANK-YOU
GUIDE

A Thoroughly Modern Manual for Expressing
Your Gratitude—Quickly, Painlessly and Personally

Sharon Naylor

A Perigee Book

THE BERKLEY PUBLISHING GROUP
Published by the Penguin Group
Penguin Group (USA) Inc.
375 Hudson Street, New York, New York 10014, USA
Penguin Group (Canada), 90 Eglinton Avenue East, Suite 700, Toronto, Ontario M4P 2Y3, Canada
(a division of Pearson Penguin Canada Inc.)
Penguin Books Ltd., 80 Strand, London WC2R 0RL, England
Penguin Group Ireland, 25 St. Stephen's Green, Dublin 2, Ireland (a division of Penguin Books Ltd.)
Penguin Group (Australia), 250 Camberwell Road, Camberwell, Victoria 3124, Australia
(a division of Pearson Australia Group Pty. Ltd.)
Penguin Books India Pvt. Ltd., 11 Community Centre, Panchsheel Park, New Delhi—110 017, India
Penguin Group (NZ), Cnr. Airborne and Rosedale Roads, Albany, Auckland 1310, New Zealand
(a division of Pearson New Zealand Ltd.)
Penguin Books (South Africa) (Pty.) Ltd., 24 Sturdee Avenue, Rosebank, Johannesburg 2196,
South Africa

Penguin Books Ltd., Registered Offices: 80 Strand, London WC2R 0RL, England

While the author has made every effort to provide accurate telephone numbers and Internet addresses at the time of publication, neither the publisher nor the author assumes any responsibility for errors, or for changes that occur after publication. Further, publisher does not have any control over and does not assume any responsibility for author or third-party websites or their content.

THE BRIDE AND GROOM THANK-YOU GUIDE

First edition: June 2006

Perigee trade paperback ISBN: 0-399-53258-7

An application to register this book for cataloging has been submitted to the Library of Congress.

PRINTED IN THE UNITED STATES OF AMERICA

10 9 8 7 6 5 4 3 2 1

This book is dedicated to
Anthony Botti, Gigi Diamond, Gary Berman and Martin Greenberg
with my thanks and love.

ACKNOWLEDGMENTS

A great big **THANK YOU** to my editors, Michelle Howry and Meg Leder at Perigee, for their guidance and enthusiasm for this project. My deepest gratitude for welcoming me to their home.

Hugs and daisies to my agent, the great Meredith Bernstein, for her unfailing support and tremendous multi-tasking, genius vision and fabulous style.

With love to my family and friends, to the newest reasons for my heart to dance, and to the sweet kindness of strangers. Michelle Norelli is one such angel I could never thank enough for her generosity of spirit, and Brianne Phillips deserves a bouquet of roses for the joy she brings to people and the good work she does in the world.

With monumental thanks to my mother, Joanne, and my father, Andy . . . true heroes to me and to all who know them.

CONTENTS

INTRODUCTION

This is an amazing time for you! You're most likely so filled with joy at the parties thrown for you, the congratulations of family and friends, the excitement of preparing for the wedding and for your future to come, that you're overwhelmed with love and happiness. Behind all that excitement, though, perhaps there's a bit of dread about the big task of writing all of those thank-you notes?

How do you express your gratitude the right way? How do you do it without sounding sappy or scripted? You're searching for the right words to say "Thank You"—to your parents, to your bridal party, to your guests, to the experts who help you plan the wedding. After all, these people helped—in small and large ways—to create the most important day of your lives. That deserves something better than a one-liner in a greeting card, right? Absolutely.

Put away the worry and the dread. We're going to make this *fun*. And efficient. You're going to get your thank-you notes written in record time, and we're going to make them extra-special by adding the secret ingredient that has been missing in thank yous from generations past.

Grooms, you're involved, too. As a full planning partner with the bride, these thank-you notes are yours to write as well. You'll team up to write them, address them, stamp them and mail them, since you've been the recipient of so much generosity and kindness as your wedding approaches, too. You'll also find your own section in this book on the thank-you notes *you'll* write for the help you receive with your tasks.

As you know, weddings have changed dramatically through the decades. People will now travel from across the globe to attend your cele-bration. The people you know and love may be more involved in help-ing to plan the wedding as their gift to you. If you have them, your kids may be involved; and of course you'll need to thank *each other* for all you're doing as a team to plan the Big Day and for all you are to one an-other as a couple.

If it sounds like you have more thank yous to write for more cate-gories, that's absolutely correct. But don't let that intimidate you. Lots of these extra thank yous can be done through e-mail or through a greeting card. So we're going to start off by making your job *easier* as we help you be the gracious bride and groom throughout the whole pro-cess.

You know it's the people behind the gifts and the favors who matter most, so that's where we're going to focus. In the upcoming pages, you'll learn ways to personalize your notes in order to add a depth of sentiment and appreciation that your guests will love. You'll also dis-cover the newest trends in thank-you categories, such as sending notes to people who couldn't attend the wedding but sent a gift anyway, thanking guests for gift cards, sending a thank you for a gift you know you'll return, thanking for gifts off your honeymoon registry or your charitable registry and more. We'll also cover ways to beat the Monot-ony Problem, presenting you with plenty of options for saying a gift is "lovely," or "useful," or "thoughtful." *The Bride and Groom Thank-You Guide* will give you everything you need to create a meaningful thank you: wording suggestions, quotes you can use, answers to all of your style questions and the freedom to talk like yourselves!

In addition to getting the wording just right, you'll also find a chap-ter on making your own thank-you notes as a budget alternative to or-dering them professionally and formally made. This book will discuss materials, layout, wording and accents, even software you can use to create custom-made thank yous that rival those other couples are spending hundreds of dollars for. You'll learn everything there is to know about how to order or make your notes—from paper styles to font colors, layouts to monograms. All to give your beautifully-written notes the perfect presentation.

And speaking of presentation, you'll also discover how to add a little something extra to your thank-you message: video of the two of you from your wedding. The newest and most exciting addition to the world of thank-you notes is sending a message, taped on your wedding day, on a DVD or video streamed onto your website. These fun videotaped messages make you the star of your own thank-you movie!

It's my pleasure and honor to help you through this process of writing your thank-you notes, as I find that this is one of the most meaningful parts of your celebration. While you have a long list of thank yous to write for so many presents, it's the love behind the list that matters most. You're so very adored by all of your family and friends. You're lucky to have so much, tangible and intangible, given to you by them all. When you write your thank-you notes with this deeper level of gratitude in mind, it will come through in what you write. And *that* is the big secret of writing unforgettable notes.

So now, dear bride and groom, let's get started. . . .

PART ONE

The Foundation of Your Thank-You Notes

Throughout your entire wedding planning process, you'll find occasion for sending many different kinds of thank-you notes—formal, informal, handwritten, even a quick e-mail "Thanks for the suggestion! We love the caterer you recommended!" A great thank you comes in many forms, whether it's a traditional treat for the recipient, such as your wedding thank-you note with portrait, or a hi-tech message, such as a DVD with a video greeting that you taped at your wedding.

It's a new world of saying thank you, and the method makes as much of an impression as the wording you use. This section will offer you a primer on selecting the right format and formality for your notes, giving you a variety of options for the many chances you'll have to show your gratitude. And since you don't want any missteps, I've included the top fifteen thank-you note mistakes to save you from any social gaffes along the way.

CHAPTER 1

Choosing Your Method

You'll send your thanks out in many different ways, depending on the circumstances. A formal, written thank-you note for a wedding gift is something that guests appreciate and expect. It's the traditional card you've seen and received yourself in the past, and the model you're most likely using for your own wedding right now.

But throughout the planning and the actual wedding ceremony, there will be *many* things to thank people for—help finding a great seamstress, a pickup at the airport, a suggestion of caterers, a kind word when you've been having a bad day, throwing you a bridal shower. Each of these wonderful gestures—all equally important to you as a person and to the success of your wedding plans—deserves a thank you, but not everything you'll receive requires a formal, written note.

While we'll get into the appropriateness of e-mail thank yous in the next chapter, for now, let's start off with the basic ways of thanking people, and which type is appropriate in which situation.

Formal Thank-You Notes

Formal thank-you notes are the ones you'd send out if you held a formal wedding, most often on white or off-white card stock with black lettering, and with an elegant design. If guests dress formally, they get this type of thank-you note.

A formal thank-you note is appropriate for:

- All the guests who attended your wedding, regardless of whether or not their gift has arrived yet. Some people do send wedding gifts after the wedding, as in the case of a custom-ordered gift that's taking longer than expected or something from your registry that hasn't been shipped. When the gift arrives, you'll send them another thank-you note. Right now, you're thanking them for what's really important: their presence on your day.

- Your wedding coordinator, who helped you pull it all together

- Your wedding experts for their fabulous work

- Guests who gave you engagement gifts

- Guests who attended your engagement party

- Guests who won't be able to attend the wedding but sent you a present anyway

Less Formal Thank-You Notes

These may look like formal thank yous with a white or ecru card stock and black lettering, but they're instantly recognizable as less formal by the wording (a more excited and playful "voice," for instance), the type of font (a more playful block lettering rather than a classic italic, for instance), perhaps a graphic, textured edges, even cutouts. A less formal thank-you note is often seen with colored card stock and colored print, as today's etiquette rules now allow for this type of expression in all wedding stationery. The difference between formal and less formal notes is subtle, but you'll be able to recognize less formal notes for their creativity of design while still bearing a message that's "up style."

A less formal thank-you note is appropriate for:

- Anyone who hosted a shower for you

- Shower guests

- Guests who couldn't attend the shower but sent a gift

- Wedding weekend event hosts

- Anyone who hosted guests staying in their homes for your wedding weekend

Thank-You Cards

If you can find a great card from a greeting card line, your work is easier for this less formal thank-you expression.

A thank-you card from the card store is appropriate for:

- Someone who helped you find your wedding vendors or locations

- Someone who volunteered to help, but hasn't done so yet. (You're thanking them for the offer.)

- Someone who is lending you items for your wedding

- Those who agreed to be in your bridal party. They're committing their time, energy and money to your wedding, so thank them now with a card in the mail.

- Someone who sent you a really nice card in the mail, either congratulating you on your engagement or just making you smile with a "thinking of you" card

The Handwritten Note

The handwritten note on a blank card is making a big comeback. Handwriting takes us back to more personal times when fonts weren't involved, and somehow the message seems to mean more when penned in the sender's unmistakable handwriting.

A handwritten note is appropriate for:

- *Any* thank-you sending, either alone or in conjunction with a gift, other than your formal, official wedding thank-you notes

- A quick note of thanks when someone has just completed a task, called with an answer or delivered on a promise early

- A quick note of thanks to someone in your household who is being supportive of the process

- Those relatives and friends who always send thoughtful handwritten notes and letters to you. You know that they favor the tradition of hand-writing their letters, so you answer in kind.

- An extra, personalized message inside a store-bought greeting card

A Thank-You Gift and Note

The rule about sending a thank-you gift is when someone's help just overwhelms you with kindness. You just don't feel like a card or note is *enough* to show your gratitude. Such gifts might include a bouquet of flowers, a bottle of fine wine, a big box of chocolates, even a gift card to a day spa or other pampering treat. When the giver has done something truly extraordinary, you might look at higher-budget items like tickets to a play or concert, a night at a boutique bed and breakfast, or the full royal treatment at that day spa. Check out gift ideas in chapter 26 for more inspiration.

A thank-you gift and note is appropriate for:

- Anyone who's gone above and beyond in helping you with the wedding, especially if their help saves you money on the wedding, such as their connecting you with a caterer who gives you a significant "Friends and Family" discount.

- A friend or relative who does something for your wedding as their wedding gift to you. This is a popular trend right now, as many people are offering to let the bride and groom use their classic car for transportation or their shore house as a reception location, their backyard garden, or their talents and skills in graphic arts or creating websites, making favors or baking desserts.

A Financial Reward and a Note

Otherwise known as giving a tip, a financial reward accompanied with a note is a wonderful extra touch. Your message may read: *With our thanks for your wonderful work!*; *We appreciate your terrific work on our (fill in the blank), and here is a little something to thank you!*; or *Thank you so much for (fill in the blank)! We'll be sure to recommend you to everyone we know.*

A financial reward and a note is appropriate for:

- All of the wedding experts you'll tip, as well as non-wedding experts like your hair stylist and babysitters who'll watch your guests' kids

Flowers and a Note

The gift of flowers will make anyone's day, but it's an especially nice thank you that goes deeper than assistance with the wedding plans alone. Especially if you choose flowers that are sentimental to the recipient, such as daisies or tulips that are their favorites, your gesture carries extra emotion.

Flowers and a note are appropriate for:

- Mothers, stepmothers, grandmothers, godmothers and other honored women for their help with the wedding. There's no better way to start off the new chapter of your life than with a bow to the people who brought you to this point.

- Wedding coordinators who really helped you. In addition to their contract fees and tip, a bouquet of roses sent after the wedding is a terrific way to add color to your "thank you."

- Your boss, for giving you extra time off for your wedding planning process and the wedding/honeymoon weeks as well.

Phone Calls

You can't lose with a phone call to say thank you, in addition to any of the thank-you note methods mentioned here. It's all in the sound of your voice, which e-mail can never duplicate. And who doesn't love getting a phone call that's not from a telemarketer, a request to serve on some volunteer committee or work-related issues?

A phone call is appropriate for:

- People who have done thoughtful tasks for you. If your sister sent over a great gift of wedding invitation software, she should get a call as well as perhaps a thank-you note and gift. If a friend flew in to attend your bridal shower, it would be appropriate if you called her for a chat in addition to sending her the same thank-you note that everyone else is getting.

- An *initial* thank you to guests who have mailed you a wedding present. Your call is to thank them in the moment, and allow them to hear your excitement, but you *must* follow up with a written thank-you note for the gift as well. This call assures them that the gift arrived on time, rather than their having to wait until months after the wedding to receive a formal thank-you note.

E-Mail Messages

E-mailed thank yous have definite advantages: They're gorgeous, they're efficient, they're free, they're easy to create, they're immediate and they'll make anyone's day. However, they shouldn't replace the official printed thank-you card. There are a few categories that *are* okay for sending informal e-mailed thank yous. Be sure to send these cute e-cards to your friends' personal e-mail accounts rather than their work accounts, as some services come with the undesirable side effect of pop-up ads, weekly junk mail or musical effects (not always ideal for the office!).

An e-mail message is appropriate for:

- Initially thanking your bridal party members—male, female and child—for agreeing to be in the bridal party. You can express your gratitude for them, and tell them there's a lot of fun ahead.

- Monthly thank yous, with cute and lighthearted graphics, to your hardworking wedding team that has shown dedication to your goals and dreams. Keep this to no more than once a month, though, as you'd otherwise cross over into the Woman Who Thanks Too Much.

- Thanking a friend for following through on a request

- Acknowledging that a friend is there for you during her own busy or rough time. Life can blindside all of us, so if your friend is having a challenge, be sure to thank her when she's still devoted to being a good team player in the bridal party.

- An affirmation after working through a problem. Choose your e-card well, one that focuses on the joy and beauty of friendship. If you've had to have a difficult conversation with a bridesmaid who wasn't following through, and your diplomatic approach and discussion went well, then it's time for a genuine thank you for partnering on a solution that saves your friendship.

- To thank your future in-laws for raising the amazing person you're marrying! Yes, you can send a pretty, interactive e-card to your sets of parents. It might be at the start of the process; not a bad way to begin on the right foot, during the hectic planning months, and especially right before the wedding.

As for expressing your thanks to one another, any of the previous categories works. I suggest you use all of them, one after the other, over time and continuing into the future, to show your gratitude for the gifts that you are to one another. It's the couples who never say thank you to each other during the planning process who have some stress issues and problems in their relationships, as the wedding crowds out the affection. Think of this as a friendly reminder for both bride and groom to make a mental note to show thanks for all you share.

CHAPTER 2

Hi-Tech Thank-You Messages

We live in a hi-tech world, and it's no wonder that the newest trend in thank-you notes is sending a thank you that *moves* and *speaks*, a hi-tech dash of style and interactive messaging. By that, I mean sending a videotaped message from the two of you—a thank you that you record on your wedding day, in your full wedding regalia, at the reception, capturing your just-married bliss—via DVD or as streaming video on your personalized wedding website.

Such thank yous are surprisingly easy to put together. At your wedding, you just need to have your videographer or a friend with a video camera tape you delivering your message of thanks (wording ideas come later in this chapter), do as many "takes" as you wish to give you the best option and then you can have that footage alone transferred to a separate DVD or to your site.

Sweating the details on how to make it happen? Don't worry. If you're not very techno-savvy, you can ask a computer-friendly friend to help you out. Or, in the case of the DVD, your videographer can take care of the task for you. That industry is moving toward the specialty-DVD trend, so you'll find plenty of opportunities for custom DVD work, labels and more.

The Thank-You Note DVD

A DVD thank you can be sent in a jewel case (the term for the plastic box that holds a DVD) with a personalized label. The recipient can then pop it into a home computer and watch your message of thanks, complete with you blowing kisses at them, smiling, waving and expressing your gratitude with that flushed-cheek excitement you have on the Big Day. Some couples record their thank-you message as they're clinking champagne flutes, and they say a little cheers to the camera (and thus, to the recipient as he or she views it).

This DVD can be a short message or it can be a professionally edited DVD masterpiece designed with titles, a musical soundtrack, a quote of your choice (see Appendix for ideas) and edited footage from the ceremony and reception. Guests *love* the ingenuity of the DVD thank-you message, and they can hold on to it for far longer than they do printed thank-you notes. They can also view it again and again, and show it to others. A DVD thank-you message also lets the receiver know that you were thinking of them on your special day, and that you were thankful in the moment.

Professionally Made DVDs

Some videographers offer packages in which they'll create DVD thank yous as part of your deal. Ask for the details. Or, you might

choose to hire a professional video-to-DVD expert, one who special-
izes in custom DVD presentations for weddings, anniversaries, corporate events, bar and bat mitzvahs, sweet sixteen parties and so on.
While your presentation won't be the usual two-hour, fully packed
movie on a disk, you'll still traverse the same world of production, editing and special features.

Many companies transfer VHS or digital footage onto DVD with
extras. They accept Digital 8, Mini DV, VHS-C and transfer to pris-
tine digital quality. Often, you'll find the option to add an opening
scene or montage (such as classical music playing while you walk
hand in hand down the beach at sunset), a title page (such as "A Message from Denise and Allen on Their Wedding Day, May 16th,
2007"), custom jewel cases (such as blush-pink translucent cases
rather than everyday clear ones) and custom labels. If you're producing
a longer DVD with your thank-you message *and* additional scenes
from the wedding with footage you've also taken from your videographer's work on the big day, these companies can give you an opening
index like you'd find on any movie DVD (minus the blooper reel, unless you choose to include that!).

As you might expect, these professionally made, custom DVDs can
run on the pricey side, but you may find it worth it for the excitement
value and uniqueness. You'll certainly find bulk discounts when you
shop around, and prices will vary depending on where you live in the
country. But you might find it a great use of some of that wedding-gift
money you'll receive.

Or, Make Them Yourselves!

It's also easy to upload video from your digital camera onto a video
editing software program, do your own edits, add your own titles and
even soundtrack and burn your own DVDs or CD-ROMs. Consider
it another project you get to work on together. Here's what you'll
need:

What If Some Guests Don't Have DVD Capabilities?

It might be surprising to you, but some people don't have home computers, or DVD players or CD-ROM drives. They're just getting used to having cell phones. You may certainly send them your DVD, though. Someone they know can load it up and show it to them. But the overriding trend is to send a printed thank-you note *along* with the DVD so that people still know they're being thanked. That card can be made on card stock on your home computer as well. Your wording would be as follows:

*With our thanks for the thrill of having you at our wedding,
and our joy for your gift, we've put a little something together
for your viewing pleasure.
Enjoy!
From our hearts to you,
Becky and Adam*

(You'll sign each printed card by hand, of course!)

- Bulk cases of DVDs

- Jewel cases (you can find unique ones at many office supply stores, craft stores or online, since DVD and CD-ROM burning is such a common practice today for corporate work as well!)

- Labels you can print at home (Avery makes a wide range of quality products found at office supply stores or online)

- Music CDs or MP3s for your soundtrack

- Boxes or padded mailers made specifically for DVD cases

- Pretty mailing labels to match your home-done DVD labels

You can expect to spend between $70 and $100 total, depending on how many DVDs you'd like to make.

Streaming Video on Your Website

If you're not familiar with the term *video stream*, it's the video that plays on a website when you click the "play" button. More and more couples are adding this easy-to-install feature to their personalized wedding websites, giving visitors the chance to watch video clips with the click of the mouse. Again, you can bring in the help of a techno-savvy friend, or hire a Webmaster just for the task of adding this feature to your site. In this way, it's a lot like hiring a wedding coordinator just to handle certain individual tasks rather than the whole wedding. Ask for referrals and bring in a computer genius who can arrange the video stream feature on your website.

You can then send a *separate* e-mail to your guests, announcing your new video stream feature and providing them with the link. This announcement, of course, would be in addition to the printed, traditional thank-you notes you'll send—personalized to the giver—as an added bonus.

It's quite important to note here that these hi-tech options are not done *in place of* traditional printed thank-you notes, but rather, *in addition* to them. Failing to do so means your messages won't be as personalized to the giver as they should be. So consider this as an extra touch to your thank-you To Do list.

The Wording for Your Video Message

You're in the moment, the party's going on all around you, and you're getting ready to film your thank-you message right there at your wedding—provided, of course, that you haven't had too much to drink! A word of advice: Tape the message early in the celebration while you still look fresh and sound coherent. Many couples choose to tape this message right after they take their post-ceremony pictures and before they enter the banquet hall. Those precious few moments of quiet and

---

Can You Do Personalized Video Messages?

Yes, you can. Just not two hundred of them, or you'll be taping all night long. Save the personalized messages for your parents, siblings, grandparents, even your bridal party. It is okay in this instance to mention all of your bridesmaids by name in one message from you, or all of your bridal party members, then make copies for all. No one will get offended at the group greeting. You can then arrange to have the different video messages transferred to DVDs, and with good organization, you can send copies to the right people.

---

privacy are perfect for taping, and you won't have to worry about guests interrupting you to hug you, or those clinking sounds signaling you to kiss (although that would be fun to capture on film, too!).

Here are some ideas for your videotaped thank-you message:

Hello! We just wanted to thank you for being a part of our wedding day! It's a dream come true for us and we're so incredibly happy right now—even more so because we got to share it with you! We send you hugs and kisses, and we'll see you soon!

or . . .

Well, we're about to walk into our reception to celebrate our marriage with everyone we love, but first we wanted to stop and say thank you for being a part of our day, for everything you've meant to us over the years and for all you bring to our lives. We're just starting our new life, and we're blessed to have you in it! We love you!

or . . .

We're married! Finally! And we're so happy that you were here to share in our big moment. Everything leading up to this time has been so amazing, and we're so thankful that you've been a part of it all. It wouldn't have been the same without you here! So thank you for making our day all the more special!

At this point, you're not thanking them for the gifts, as at the time of your taping, you haven't opened them yet! So save that for your hand-written thank-you notes. Instead, you're thanking your friends and relatives for their presence and how much they mean to you as part of your circle of loved ones. That's the big message.

CHAPTER 3

The Top 15
Thank-You Mistakes

No matter which types of thank-you notes you decide to use in each situation, the most important thing to keep in mind—and probably a large portion of the reason you bought this book—is avoiding making any mistakes within your thank-you notes! While of course you want to sound great with your wording, it's perhaps even more important to sidestep any unforeseen errors or slights that may hurt someone's feelings or make you look bad. Writing thank yous is the very last step of your wedding adventure. It would be a shame to do so much well and right all along and then make an unintentional mistake now. The top fifteen mistakes to watch out for are:

1. *Going generic.* "Thank you for your generous gift" has no flair, no feeling, no depth. Instead, try mixing up your wording from

note to note, as some of your guests may see others' notes on their countertops or posted on their refrigerators. Adding a little personality to your notes not only makes it more fun for you, you'll show your guests that you took the time to personalize your messages to them. Need help with wording? Check out the Thank-You-Note Thesaurus in the Appendix for suggestions.

2. *Sending the same exact message to everyone on your list.* Yes, you turned "thank you for your generous gift" into something creative and sentimental, but you've stopped right there and used it on all two hundred thank-you notes. Remember that guests often see each other's cards, and no one wants a "duplicate gift" in the wording you use. Mix it up a little bit and personalize your notes even further.

3. *Saying "Thank you for the gift," but nothing else.* That mistake can make you look materialistic, as if the gift they gave is the only thing that counts for you. Instead, consider also focusing on how much you loved having them there for your day as well, or anything else personalized about them as people. Compliment the dress she was wearing. Tell him he can really move on the dance floor. Let them know you loved seeing them right after the ceremony. It's about the experience shared with them, not just what was in the box or envelope they gave you.

4. *Printing the entire thing out on the computer, including your signatures.* While you can of course print out the wording of your thank-you note, you should always sign by hand.

5. *Waiting way too long to send your thank-you notes.* Granted, it can take months for your wedding portraits to come in, and guests know this. A few months' delay is understandable if you're including a photo with your notes, but nine months and no word from you? That's a breach of etiquette and makes you look like you don't feel the need to say thank you.

6. *Forgetting some people.* Be organized. Use your original guest list and send a thank-you note to everyone on it. It's a big mistake to use only a collection of the cards you received, as by their nature some can get lost. When a guest is the only one not to receive a thank-you note, that's trouble waiting to happen.

7. *Getting a guest's gift wrong.* Ouch! You thanked the McParlands for the beautiful tea set, but they gave you a set of Bordeaux glasses . . . that they shipped home from France. Keep good records, and if you're not sure of the gift they gave, use less specific language.

8. *Not putting all the givers' names on the cards.* If the gift was from Jack and Karen and their three kids Micah, Leslie, and Simon, then they all should be mentioned on the card, even if you know eight-month-old Simon had nothing to do with the choice of present.

9. *Making it too obvious that you don't know what they gave you.* If you don't have a record of a giver's present—but you know that they did indeed give you something, not that the gift will be shipped later—you'll still need to find a way to avoid that cookie-cutter "Thank you for the generous gift!" message. (This could backfire on you when the giver *knows* the gift he or she gave wasn't exactly generous.) You can word vaguely with talent, such as saying "We thank you for the gift, and more important, we loved spending time with you." Yes, you skimmed over the gift topic, but sometimes you have no choice. If no one around you remembers what that particular gift was, you'll want to refocus your thank-you note with honest appreciation for their gift-giving gesture, and then be completely genuine about the other elements of the thank-you note. Never try to bluff, and never make the mistake of being too vague: "What you gave us was so interesting!"

10. *Using the word interesting.* Years of wedding industry talk has proven that the word *interesting*, used to describe a cake taste, a song or a wedding gift, generally means that you couldn't come up with anything positive to say about it.

11. *Mentioning the dollar amount the cash-givers gave you.* This isn't a receipt, so you don't have to put the exact dollar amount. This is a subtle mistake, which we'll discuss further in chapter 8 on thanking guests for cash gifts.

12. *Putting a picture in some thank-you notes but not others.* Again, guests do see each other's cards, and they'll inevitably talk about the great picture you enclosed. It can hurt a guest's feelings if it appears that you chose to include a photo of yourselves only for "special" guests, such as the big-spenders. Yes, it seems like a little thing, but guests really do get offended when they don't get a picture like everyone else.

13. *Sending one catch-all thank-you note for a range of events, like showers and the bachelorette party.* Each event requires its own card. Efficiency isn't an option here.

14. *Bragging about how many presents you received.* You may not realize it, maybe you're just really excited about the sheer elegance and exorbitance of the gifts you received, but it can sound very tacky in black and white. "We can't believe all the wonderful things we got! Everyone should be so lucky!" is just not the best way to thank someone for the salt and pepper shakers.

15. *Signing only one of your names, speaking for both of you.* The thank-you note should always be from the two of you, even if one of you did the actual writing and signing. You're a "We" now, especially for this task, so both of your names go on the card.

PART TWO

Saying Thank You...
for the Gifts

How do you thank someone for a gift card they've given you off your registry? Or for the champagne cruise they got you from your honeymoon registry? How do you thank someone for a cash gift? Or for that ugly vase you plan to return? In this section, you'll find out the rules and phrasing suggestions for the kinds of gifts you may receive (although hopefully not that ugly vase!).

No gift is more valuable than another, of course. They all come from the givers' hearts. Yet how do you word the thank-you note when you don't know what you'll get with the gift card, or when some people gave a higher denomination of cash than others? How can you make a thank-you for that blender more interesting? You'll find all the guidance you need right here . . .

CHAPTER 4

Engagement Gifts

There are several types of engagement parties these days. Of course, the most popular is the traditional scenario, where your parents host a fabulous soiree for you, attended by all relatives, your friends, their friends, colleagues, bosses and people who really don't know you. The big engagement party is a reason to welcome in the great news of your family, and like brides and grooms of decades past, there's a lot to be thankful for in the form of shared enthusiasm and a few tables' worth of beautifully wrapped presents.

Another type of engagement party comes in the form thrown by friends—a big trend now that we're more of a global society. We don't always live in the same hometown as our parents. We've moved to the city or across the country for work or for love, and we have a circle of loved ones in our "adopted hometown." Thus, the engagement party hosted by a local friend, work friends, the people in your building . . . or four separate parties thrown by each group.

However, not every couple has an engagement party. In recent years, more couples have chosen to skip the big guest list engagement bash in favor of a smaller dinner or at-home celebration with close family and friends. Since this is a relatively new trend, some of your guests might be confused about etiquette rules: Are they supposed to send an engagement gift to you if there's no party? And how should you thank them for such a gift?

This chapter will provide you with thank-you wording for any scenario. Regardless of the type of party thrown for you, who hosts it, or where it's held, this is your first opportunity to say thank you in style. Use the following examples to guide the formality and wording, to figure out when you need to be classic and when you can use some humor and how to thank your hosts for the party in addition to the gift they gave you.

Essential Extra Details Within Your Notes

Within your engagement party thank-you notes, you'll let your guest know why you love the gift, how you're using it *now*, and how it helps you in some way. Guests love knowing they've gotten you something you can really enjoy, and it's extra points when their gift helps you prepare for the wedding . . . or brings you a romantic moment. Always let them know that in addition, you loved spending time with them, that you appreciated their coming to the engagement party and you can't wait to see them at the wedding—and afterwards. Let them know their gift has you excited about the future, and that they'll be a part of it . . . that's the best thank-you message possible at the start of your engagement time.

Formal Parties

When a formal party has been given in your honor, as described in chapter 1, your thank-you notes will conform to the level of the party's formality. That means you'll choose a classic style for your thank-you notes to match the formality of the invitations sent *for* the engagement party (no matter your chosen source for either ordering or making them), but more important, your language will be more formal as well. That means a light, airy, humorous tone is not quite right for this style of event. When the party is upscale, simply referring to elements of it will lift your note into the appropriate tone.

Look through the Thesaurus section in the Appendix for words that are more formal, such as *elegant, lovely, masterful,* and incorporate these into your notes. The examples on the following pages show a range of formal styles, for instance. The first includes reference to the formality of the party itself, and the others convey their formality in the straightforward style of language mixed with personalized elements like future invitations to spend time together.

Formality simply connotes that your thank-you notes are direct, without jokes or smiley-face icons, and that they include proper greetings and closers (see the Thesaurus for suggestions). This style is what most often comes to mind when you think "thank-you notes," and they are indeed a call to those traditional times when all thank-you correspondence carried an air of society, respectful greetings and considerate details. So find your formal voice. Practice a bit before you begin to match proper formality with your own expression style so that you don't sound too stilted or awkward. An insider secret: Use a style that's close to the proper wording you'd use in an important business letter, filled with details and just the right dose of your personality.

Look at the samples here to see how a formal thank-you note looks in this category . . . nothing too obvious stands out, but the *words* you choose do all the work for you. For instance, you'll use "Thank you" rather than "Thanks" at the opener of your letter; it's simply a more formal shade of gratitude.

Dear Sarah and Tom,

Thank you for the beautiful candlesticks! Now we can have romantic dinners at home by candlelight while we plan the wedding! It was lovely to spend time with you at the engagement party, and we'll hope to spend more time with you at the wedding! Thank you again, and we'll see you soon.

Love,
Angie and Bob

Dear Monica, Tom, Peter and Chelsea,

Thank you so much for coming to our engagement party! We haven't seen you in so long that it only made it all the more special that you were there. Thanks, too, for the wineglasses set—the first toast will be said in your honor! Here's hoping that we'll have a chance to get together soon, and we'll see you at the wedding.

Love,
Renee and Mark

Dear Aunt Tamika and Uncle Roy,

Thank you so much for the gorgeous platter! You always have such amazing taste, and it's perfect for our dining room table. We're so excited about seeing you at the wedding, and we're glad that we could start our "wedding planning season" off with such wonderful family like you.

All our love,
Micah and Henry

Informal Gatherings with Close Family and Friends

When the event you've shared was a smaller, more intimate get-together as opposed to a formal bash with invitations and a catered menu, your thank-you note will match the formality of the event. You'll use the same gracious tone as you would for any size of party, but when the event is less formal, you can write in a more "conversational" tone rather than a more professional, proper tone. (If you're not sure of what your written "conversational" tone is, do some practicing. Speak aloud what you'd say to a guest at the close of the party, and then write that down. See how your language works in a more informal way?)

Mention details, such as toasts made, songs sung, quiet moments spent alone with friends and family. These informal situations lend themselves perfectly to your expressing why the smaller, more intimate party atmosphere gave you more of what you really value: time with the giver.

The gift itself may also play into the theme, allowing you to plan future informal, smaller or more intimate gatherings with your loved ones; if that's the case, be sure to promise future invitations as well.

As for your style of thank-you note, handwritten notes work just fine for this type of gathering, as do store-bought thank-you cards (either classic or humorous, priceless if they refer to some element that was contained in the party, such as a poolside location.

Look at the examples below and compare them to the more formally worded notes on pages 32 to 33. You'll notice a difference in the conversational tone, the words chosen and the lighter style.

Dear Georgette,

How great a party was that! We were so thrilled to be able to celebrate in style with you, and you definitely made our night with that rendition of "Moon River!" Thank you so much for the cashmere throw blanket . . . You've just made it easier for Rob to set up romantic midnight picnics by the fireplace, so we both thank you for your help with our love life! We'll see you soon, and thank you again for making our party unforgettable.

Love,
Sasha and Rob

Dear Danielle and Warren,

Thank you, thank you, thank you for the martini set! We've been talking for a long time about wanting to throw great cocktail parties here at our place, and you'll be the first ones on our guest list! We'll drink a toast to you now, and we'll see you very soon. Next time, dinner will be at our place! Say hello to Spencer and Max for us.

Love,
Tara and Kenneth

Dear George,

We're just floored! Where did you find the Egyptian prints?! Major points for remembering that we've always wanted to go to Cairo, and now you've just given us a great idea for our honeymoon! Thank you so much for the inspiring gift, and for making our party so much fun! You tell a great joke! We can't wait to see you again at the shore house this summer, and we thank you again for the amazing artwork. We've put them up in our living room, and everyone asks us about them. You're making us look good! ☺

Love,
Eileen and John

Dear Jessica and Jarret,

Thank you so much for the espresso maker! Now we'll have an energy boost whenever we need it to plan the wedding! We're so glad we had the chance to spend time with you at the party—wasn't it great ending the night with a bottle of wine by the pool? We'll remember it always. If only we had more quiet times like that to talk and catch up. It's always a blast hanging out with you, and we just love it that you were there. Thank you.

Love,
Anna and Ben

Dear Juliet,

Now those were some great margaritas! Thanks for being at our party—it wouldn't have been as much fun without you there, and we know the bartender will never forget you! Please tell us you're going to call him! Thank you so much for the towel set, too. While we can't say we'll be thinking of you while we use them (ha, ha) we're definitely thrilled that you got them for us. Maybe when you and the bartender house-sit for us during the honeymoon . . . hmmmmm . . . (did we mention we hope you'll call him? ☺) We love you and we thank you for making our party unforgettable!

Love,
Claire and Harold

When There Is No Party, But You Get a Gift Anyway

In some family circles, it's now become a choice *not* to hold engagement parties or pre-wedding events. Some folks don't want to obligate their loved ones to give extra gifts, or to travel, and sometimes the bride and groom just aren't living nearby to make it convenient to hold a party in their honor. Still, some people may send gifts as their own tradition, party or no party. When they do, it's from their heart, and your thank-you note will show the joy their gift brought to you. I've included a sample here to show you how to mention the gift, what the moment of opening was like, and how you're looking forward to seeing the giver and expressing thanks in person in the future.

Dear Jen and Trey,

Thank you so much for the fiestaware set! It was such a surprise to find that package waiting for us at home when we returned from Thanksgiving. We wish we could have gotten out to celebrate with all of you back home, but we'll make sure we make up for it at the wedding! It was so thoughtful of you to send us a gift as we start on this exciting path, and we have even bigger smiles on our faces now, thanks to you! We'll see you soon and send you hugs across the miles!

Love,
Tina and George

The Combination
Gift-and-Hosting Thank You

Of course, you'll thank your parties' hosts for honoring you with the celebration in a smooth and natural flow that includes both the gift they gave and the experience of the party itself. Since the *experience* is always more valuable than the gift, you should mention that first in your note.

Dear Mom and Dad,

Thank you so much for giving us such a beautiful engagement party! Everything was perfect, right down to the éclairs and chocolate-covered strawberries. Everyone raved about what great parties you throw, and it was so unbelievably special to us that we could celebrate at home in such fine style. We appreciate everything you did to make the night special for us . . . we'll never forget it. And thank you for the champagne glasses set. The first thing we're going to toast is having such wonderful parents. We're so lucky to get to share this exciting time, and all the wedding preparations coming up, with you.

We love you very much,
Dana and Edward

Dear Dad and Tracy,

Thank you so much for giving us such a gorgeous engagement party! The flowers were beautiful, the food was amazing and we especially loved the music mix you made. Every song brought back great family memories. It meant so much to have you create that for us. And a great big thank you for the patio set! We're so excited that our backyard oasis is almost complete, and we'll soon be hosting you at our parties. We can't thank you enough for giving us this great celebration, as it means so much to us to spend time with our family and friends. You made it possible for us to celebrate in style with so many of our nearest and dearest, which is the best gift we could hope for.

We love you,
Paula and Jack

Dear Carrie,

Wow, what an amazing party! Thank you so much for everything you did to put that great night together. That dessert bar was incredible, and everyone is still raving about it. We can't thank you enough for giving us that experience, and you've certainly gotten us off on the right foot as we start to plan the wedding (finally!). Now we know who to call about the desserts we'll have at the reception! And thank you as well for the panini machine. Of course our most talented gourmet chef friend would help us have some talent in the kitchen! We love it and we'll use it for many a midnight snack and picnic. Again, thank you so much, Carrie. You've made us unbelievably happy and excited about all the plans to come.

Love,
Sherry and Mike

Dear Grandma and Grandpa,

Thank you so much for giving us such a beautiful garden tea party. It meant so much to us to celebrate in your garden, where I have so many happy family memories. We loved everything about it, but most of all the fact that it was with you. Everything was just beautiful, and Grandpa, you make a terrific bellini! Everyone was raving about how elegant the party was, and we couldn't be happier about sharing the day with all of our family and friends. So thank you for giving us such a wonderful start to our exciting adventure ahead. And thank you, thank you, thank you for the silver tea service. I have a feeling you'll be seeing that again at your 75th anniversary party! We'd like to host it. We love you very much, and we're very blessed to have you in our lives.

Love,
Annika and Charles

CHAPTER 5

Shower Gifts

Shower gifts are, by nature, your loved ones' way of "setting you up" for the future. You've undoubtedly registered for what you want, as a matter of efficiency and to help your guests meet their goal: getting you the things you need. Since we're no longer in a society where all brides and grooms are starting from scratch and setting up their first households ever, shower gifts have changed from just the essentials to more stylish items, luxury items and upgrades to what you already have. Shower gifts today allow you to improve the quality of your everyday items.

You may be combining two full his-and-hers households, so your gifts will also include "blending" items to weave your styles together, organizational items like baskets and closet systems, home improvement items and hi-tech treats like plasma screen TVs and home security systems. While the items on your registry list may be different than those your mother had on her list, the need to send thanks for your many,

many acquisitions has not changed in level of gratitude. It's the one thing that never changes: a great thank you that expresses your pleasure with the gift, and acknowledges the giver's generosity.

The Gift of Great Shower Gift Thank-You Notes

As an added message in today's shower thank-you notes, you'll share how the gift will be used, how it will enhance your life or meet your goals, how it supports the passion of your marriage, even how it will give you the gift, over and over, of sharing time with friends and loved ones. This is especially true when the gift in question is of a party nature, such as a margarita mixer or slow cooker for those great winter stews. The big focus of today's shower gifts is on home and hearth, creating a wonderful shared environment and entertaining friends and family at your place. Your thank-you notes, then, should reflect that your guests have helped to give you a *lifestyle*, not just an item in your cupboard. You're thanking them for making *that* possible. Each teacup, wineglass, cheese board, cappuccino machine, tablecloth and bed sheet . . . it all creates your dream home life.

Avoid the Most Common Shower Gift Thank-You Mistake

If you thank someone for the teapot that *you* registered for, saying only that the teapot is so cute and fabulous, aren't you really just complimenting your own taste in selecting it? Always be sure to thank the giver for what the teapot allows you to do, not just for it as an item. Take the next step with your expression; guests do notice what you focus on in your thank-you note. Instead, consider mentioning how you'll make it a part of your future family brunches or book club gatherings, Sunday morning paper-reading or tea parties you'll plan with your nieces.

Sharing the Emotion

Share what you felt when you opened the gift, and how wonderful it was to do so in the giver's presence. This is very important, as many of your gifts will be opened in private. The giver was sitting there when you unwrapped that luggage set, and she saw your joy. You looked around the room to make eye contact with her, and you may have winked or blown her a kiss of thanks. In today's thank-you notes, you'll incorporate that *moment*, and expand on it:

> *Oh, Terri, I don't know if you could see from where you were, but I absolutely had tears in my eyes over your great gift of the luggage. Gary and I were really hoping to get a matching set, and this means so much to us. I'm sorry I couldn't hop up and give you a hug right then, but I'll get you the next time I see you.*

You've just incorporated your in-the-moment emotion in your thank-you note for a shower gift opened in the giver's presence.

Additional Things to Thank For

At many showers, you'll also receive additional gifts, such as printed recipes or "Wishing Well" items (for those of you not in regions where this is practiced, hosts either make or rent a wishing well and fill it with small household items like spices and cotton balls, anything tiny and essential for the home). Even though you'll have no idea who gave you the great set of spices or the fun emery boards, you should still add a line of thanks for how fun it was to get those Wishing Well items.

And finally, a shower is much more than a few hours' worth of opening gifts. There are party games and toasts to thank for as well, so be sure to find out who brought that fabulous game along that everyone loved so much and add a note of thanks for that.

Shower Gifts from Those Who Couldn't Attend

Some of your loved ones who couldn't make it to the shower may send a gift in their absence. That means that part of your wonderful thank-you note will go beyond thanking them for the gift they selected, or the gift card sent in a greeting card (as is often the case for ease of shipping) and share some details of the day. Let them know not just that everyone had fun, but how lovely a day it was for a garden tea party. Share some of the memorable moments. Let them know they were missed and that you look forward to showing them pictures. Some brides and grooms are also offering to e-mail digital images from the party if the giver would like to see. That's a terrific way to take your thank-you notes one step further, by sharing the experience. And of course, make mention of the fact that you appreciate them thinking of you even though they couldn't be there in person. If you proposed a toast to them in their absence, as some parties do, mention that as well.

How Do You Sign a Shower Thank-You Note?

If you're the guest of honor at a traditional females-only bridal shower, you might think that the thank you would be from you alone. After all, the guests made out their cards to you, right? It used to be that way, but not anymore. Now, even if the shower is just for you, the bride-to-be, and even if the cards are made out to just you, you'll sign the thank-you note from both of you. After all, you registered for gifts together, and you'll both be using the items you receive. So add the groom's name and an expression of how he, too, will enjoy the sauté pans, the throw pillows, the fireplace set. It's not an insult to a guest who followed habit and addressed the card to you; it's simply a gentle glide into the new way of things where bride and groom are equals.

For co-ed bridal showers, men and women celebrate together, giving or opening gifts together as well. At these parties, it's even more clear that the message of gratitude for your home dream-come-true will come from the two of you. Either you can sign each card in your own handwriting, or one of you can sign both of your names. Both options are fine.

Shower Gifts from Children

Kids' notes are a joy to write. Sure, it may be that the parents picked out the gift to be given in the flower girls' names, but it's smart etiquette for you to send a separate thank-you note addressed to the children themselves. Kids love getting mail, so your note directly to them will be appreciated. Again, thank them for the gift and for any part they may have played in the planning of the party. Compliments on their party dresses are always welcome. The same goes for ring bearers if they are a part of a co-ed shower.

Look at the examples on the pages to follow to see just how these rules for shower gift thank yous read in real life. Star, circle or flag any phrasing that sounds great to you, and feel free to use these models as your own shower gift thank-you notes.

For Home Essentials

Home essentials are those wonderfully welcome home décor items, kitchen appliances and gadgets, furniture and the makings of your future home. Your guests had their choice of which kind of gift to get you, and they made the choice to give you an item you will use every day or on special occasions. Their gift becomes a part of your daily routine, or perhaps even starts a new family tradition.

Dear Leslie,

Thank you so much for the coffeemaker! Now we don't have to stand in line at the coffeehouse every morning, so thanks to you, Bill and I can find much better ways to spend our mornings. ☺ It was terrific to see you again at the shower, and we'll be talking with you soon to set up that dinner date.

Love,
Emily and Bill

Dear Aunt Carole,

We can't thank you enough for getting our entire bedding set! It was the #1 thing on our list, and we're so grateful that you indulged us with our most wished-for things. It was lovely to see you at the shower, and so great to see the photos of Daniel and Maria's new baby! Can't wait to see you again, and get ready for a terrific time at the wedding!

Love,
Kelly and Tom

Dear Aunt Shaye and Lucy,

We can't thank you enough for the cookware set! We've already given it a place of honor in our cabinets, and I'm looking at all the great new recipes we'll be trying out together. So thank you for giving us the gift of fun dinner nights at home, and I'm sure we'll be cooking a meal for you here sometime in the near future! It was great to spend time with you at the shower (and Lucy, excellent job at the shower games!), and we'll see you very soon.

Love,
Tara and Brian

For Luxury Items

No blenders here! Your guests have decided to skip the essentials and shower you with the luxuries on your list, including pampering items like baskets of massage oils and pedicure sets, spa robes, bathtub pillows and those cashmere blankets for the bed or couch. Their aim was to make your life indulgent, and they succeeded tremendously. So you'll thank them in a slightly different way, while keeping the details of just how romantic you plan to be with those cashmere blankets discreetly to yourself. But you *can* hint at it . . .

Dear Jane,

Thank you, thank you, thank you for the cashmere blanket! It was one of those things that we thought "if only" when we chose it, and we almost didn't expect to receive it. But thanks to you, we have our most luxurious gift, and we can't get enough of it. You've made our day! Great to see you at the shower, and we'll be seeing you very soon at Marcia and Ben's wedding in a few weeks. Prepare for a big hug of thanks from us!

Love,
Jennie and Todd

Dear Aunt Wendy,

Wow, we still can't get over the spa set you gave us! We just love the silk robes and slippers, and we've already set up the fountain shower-head. You've turned our little bathroom into a relaxing spa! The soaps and oils are just amazing . . . perfect for blissing out after a long day (and all these wedding plans!). It was terrific to see you at the shower, and we would love to have you join us at the ski house sometime this winter. Thanks again for spoiling us with such great gifts!

Love,
Eve and Jorge

Group Gifts

Very often, a luxury gift will be given by a group, such as all of your bridesmaids or all of the groomsmen, the entire bridal party, or both sets of parents. Families might join together to get you something big from your registry list, such as a barbecue grill or that plasma screen television. When this happens, and it likely will, you'll send a separate thank-you note *to each giver* for making this dream of yours come true. Just be sure to avoid the most common pitfall in this new breed of thank-you note, which is thanking them for "your share of" the gift. Yes, we all know they kicked in a percentage, but you're not to delineate like that. No one is ever thanked for partly giving you anything. Instead, you'll word your thank you more subtly, like so:

Dear Jennifer,

We're still floored by your gift! Thank you so much for the plasma screen television! We haven't smiled like that since the night we got engaged, so thank you for giving us such an amazing surprise. You're so invited over to our place for movie night, and we claim the Super Bowl party this year! It was great to see you at the shower, and we'll be seeing you soon!

Love,
Dina and Gregg

Dear Mom and Dad,

We can't thank you enough for the home office furniture! What an amazing present to support our new business like this, and we love, love, love the leather office chairs. The first thing we're placing on the desk, though, is that family photo of all of us from Cape Cod. It wouldn't be our "second home" without it! And thank you for everything, all the way through . . . we love you with all our hearts . . .

Tina and Bryan

For "Upgrades"

It's a bit tacky to say "Wow, this is *so* much better than the crappy knife set we've had for ten years!" However, you can thank the giver for upgrading your old things and be honest about how happy you are to have "the good stuff." It's a given that if you're registering for a coffeemaker with grinder, timer and talking reminder system, you're obviously upgrading the old hand press you've used during your single years. But thank-you notes are for real expressions! You can be honest about how thrilled you are to have a better version of coffeemaker for the better version of your life. Here are some examples of the subtle wording, and sense of humor, that's appropriate when you're acknowledging an appreciated upgrade:

A Note About Knife Thank Yous

Believe it or not, I've heard from an increasing number of wedding guests with funny stories about thank-you notes received for cutlery gifts. The comment *"Thank you so much for the knife set! We can't wait to have you over for dinner!"* is striking some as either quite hilarious or somewhat creepy . . . in a Hannibal Lecter kind of way. So watch out for your phrasing when you're thanking for knives or knife sharpeners!

Dear Aunt Minnie,

Thank you so much for the carving knife set! No more shredded turkey on Thanksgiving, thanks to you! ☺ We just love it, and now of course we're looking for great new recipes to try. We really appreciate your making our time in the kitchen sooo much easier now. It was wonderful to see you at the shower—you look terrific, by the way!—and we'll see you very soon.

Love,
Melanie and Frank

Tying in the Recipe Cards

At many showers, hosts ask the guests to bring along their favorite family recipes on cards for the bride and groom. If you've received recipe cards as part of your "home building" celebration, be sure to find a way to tie them into your thank-you note, too, especially if someone has taken the time and trouble to write out a great recipe by hand for you. Thank them for their efforts.

Dear Sarah and Jaime,

Thank you so much for the cookware set! Now all of our pots and pans match, finally! ☺ *We love them and have already started using them. . . . You'll have to come by for dinner some night soon. Great to see you again, and thank you also for the fabulous recipes! That teriyaki shrimp dish sounds divine! We'll see you soon~*

Love,
Jill and Everett

Dear Mya,

We LOVE the suitcases! You're sending us off on our honeymoon in style, and we were just talking about how we now feel like a "real married couple" with matching suitcases, after traveling for years with his brown ones and my blue ones. Now we match, thanks to you! We can't thank you enough for adding the monograms, too—what a great surprise! It was great to spend time with you at the shower, and let's plan a beach weekend soon, okay?

Love you lots,
Anne Marie and Dennis

For Romantic Items

Lingerie, marabou heels, massage oils, books about having great sex . . . a big trend in shower gifts is giving a little something *else* for the bedroom in the form of romantic or sexy presents. It's the gift that keeps on giving, say many shower guests, and smiling (or blushing) brides and grooms agree.

Your task now is to word your thank-you notes appropriately, and this may be the category that presents the biggest challenge for couples. If part of great thank-you-note writing includes telling guests how you plan to use the item, or how it's made your lives better, you can't exactly go into detail the way you would with that luggage set. Save the commentary about how great your breasts look in that corset for happy hour with the girls . . .

Dear Tania,

Thank you so much for the gorgeous lingerie! Needless to say, we both appreciate your great choice and you have just started off my married-girl collection in style. So a great big thank you from us both. *Fabulous to see you again, and thanks also for putting together the shower for us. You're the best!*

Love,
Aimee and Kyle

Dear Veronica,

Excellent gift! Thanks so much for the basket of massage oils and lotions, and especially those massage cards with different techniques for each day. We SO owe you a dinner out in exchange for the hours of relaxing we're getting from your present. Thanks for getting us the perfect gift! We loved seeing you at the shower, and we'll see you soon!

All our love,
Sherry and Ahmad

Are Smiley Faces Okay?

Yes! They may be a Don't for business e-mails, but it's perfectly fine for you to pen in your artistic rendering of the smiley-face emoticon as a way to convey a joke or the fact that you're smiling as you write. It's doubtful anyone has ever thrown away or burned a thank-you note because it has a smiley face on it (even a quick hand-drawn smiley at the bottom of a formal thank-you note), so feel free to show your happiness with fun and friendly art.

Dear Ellen,

We LOVE the romantic classics DVDs! Thank you so much for starting off our collection with such great films, and the bottle of wine is only going to make our first movie night all the better! Syrahs are our favorite, by the way, so you just brought us back to that wine country weekend where we got engaged! Nice touch. ☺ It was great catching up with you at the shower, and we're so glad you can come to the wedding! We'll see you soon and thanks again for the fabulous gift basket. We love it!

Love,
Steve and Debbie

For Co-Ed Shower Thank-You Notes

In instances where the shower is thrown for you as a couple, then you may *both* write the thank-you notes. Some will be from the bride and some will be from the groom. What else could better convey the equality in a partnership?

The shower gift thank-you examples shown in this chapter thus far were, of course, written by the bride because the party was thrown for her. She was the guest of honor, she opened the gifts, and she rightly

To Give You Both More Incentive . . .

Designate a reward for after your thank-you-note-writing sessions. It could be going out for a drink afterwards, going out for dinner or dessert or couple's massages, a shared bubble bath or full-scale seduction when the last stamp for the evening is affixed. Get creative with your rewards, and you'll both look forward even more to these evenings.

wrote out the thank-you notes as the Bearer of the "We." Meaning, she wrote the note for herself and her groom. That is standard protocol now. But when the party is for the bride *and* groom, he gets to pick up the pen as well.

Many couples sit down together and split the list for co-ed parties. You might want to plan thank-you-note-writing dinners/quiet evenings at home, with a set number of notes to write in each session. Keep your numbers on the low side to give yourselves a more realistic time frame, allowing you both to really focus on the task at hand. It's a mistake to expect that you'll both get all of the notes written in one session, unless your shower was very small and there are only twenty or so notes to write. So get out your schedules and set up times to pen a dozen or so thank-you notes each on several different nights or weekend days. See the Appendix for more on creating your writing timetable, and check out the co-ed shower thank-you note examples below.

No "Love"?

It's a matter of choice on how you wish to sign off on your letters. Look at "Your Thank-You-Note Thesaurus" in the Appendix for different possibilities—especially how *not* to close off your note. For now, know that it's perfectly okay to skip the "Love," before your names if you don't regularly sign notes to people that way.

Dear Helen and Tim,

Great to see you at the party last weekend, and thanks for the DVD organizer system. Movie night is at our place sometime soon, and now we'll be able to quickly eliminate the romantic comedies! Seriously, though, we were really happy to get your gift, and we've already set it up. It looks great and makes us seem somewhat organized now. Great choice. We'll see you at the wedding, and thanks again—

Bob and Sarah

Dear Mom and Dad,

Thank you so much for the barbecue grill and cookware set. We really appreciate your making it possible for us to complete our outside deck, and you're first on the guest list for our first cookout after the honeymoon. It was our most-wanted gift and we can't wait for all the family parties to come. Everything you've done for us this past year has meant so much, and we just want to say how grateful we are. We're lucky to have you.

Love,
Paul and Lainie

Dear Alex and Kim,

Great party! Thanks for hosting, and we had a blast! Thanks for the closet system—it was the one thing we really needed as we move in together. Excellent gift, and we're enjoying setting it up. We'll give you a call for happy hour sometime soon, and we'll see you next month at the wedding.

Todd and Becky

CHAPTER 6

Gift Cards

If you've registered for gift cards to your favorite stores and online sites, you've probably received more than a few. Guests say they love buying gift cards rather than big, wrapped gifts because they're able to help the bride and groom get the essentials they still need after the shower. Even in a somewhat small denomination, those gift cards can be bunched together to buy that $500 bedding set or a DVD player. It's a win-win, and that's why more couples are registering for gift cards as well.

So what are the keys to writing a fantastic thank-you note for something as "open" as a gift card? It's precisely that openness that presents a challenge in thank-you-note-writing world. What they've given you is the gift to make your own choices; that alone can add an extra dimension to your thank-you note.

The Openness Factor

The openness factor may be the best part of the gift. You get to walk into your favorite stores armed with a handful of gift cards, in all kinds of denominations, and fill your shopping cart with your favorite things. Even better, if you have a completion program on your gift registry—allowing you discounts on anything your guests didn't buy off the list—you receive *discounts* on those items, so you get even more. It's quite a fun day for a bride and groom to get what is essentially a free shopping spree in their dream store, and your guests would love to hear about how much fun you had as well as how you loaded up on all those fun kitchen gadgets and bedroom accents, how the groom got the wet-vac he's been drooling over and how the experience itself (No guilt! No credit card balances!) made for an unforgettable day. The giver(s) will love just picturing you in the store, practically skipping and maybe even doing a Happy Dance or two.

Sharing the Details

When you receive gift cards, your thank-you note is going to contain the obvious added benefit: You'll let the guest know what you bought with their gift. Guests love finding out what they contributed to, as it was their intention to give you the very excitement and happiness you'll convey in your note. Never be vague, stopping at "We got just what we needed!" Talk about the bedding set. Talk about how great it was to get the last one on the shelf. Tell them the extra-wide bagel toaster is just what you wanted. Be specific and share your enthusiasm! If you haven't yet used the gift cards, you can let the giver know what you plan to get.

Give Them an Image of the Item in Your Home

Again, guests want to know how their gift card added to your home environment, or to the experiences you have within it. So wherever you can, give them a description of what your choices added to your place. Imagine how excited they will be for you when you tell them you're sitting in front of your fireplace right now, with the throw blanket over the two of you as you write your thank-you notes. You've just shown the giver that your choice with their gift card gave you that scenario. They'll smile for you just thinking about it.

Let Them Know They'll See It, Too

The word *experience* is popping up all over this book, so it's no surprise to you that a key element in a thank you for a gift card is not just sharing what you chose, but promising that your gift will play a part in future family parties, dinners at your place, cocktail parties or tailgate parties. The new world of thank-you notes takes it a step further by inviting the giver to future *experiences* with you so that they may enjoy the gift they got you as well.

Dear Jerri,

Thank you so much for the gift card! We now have our much-wished-for window treatments with amethyst finials! We just loved picking them out, and we can't thank you enough for your present . . . and for being at the shower. It was terrific to see you after so long, and let's plan a dinner sometime soon!

Love,
Alyah and Gary

Dear Michelle,

Thank you, thank you, thank you for the big gift card! We had a blast in the kitchen section of Bed Bath & Beyond, and I think we got every kind of utensil and gadget possible! Who knew they even made avocado peelers?! That was the most fun we've ever had in a store, and you made it possible. So now we'd like to invite you over for lunch, where perfectly peeled avocados will be on the menu! Great to see you again at the shower, and we'll see you at the wedding!

Love,
Talia and Igor

Dear Warren and Magda,

Wonderful to see you both again at the shower! We're so appreciative that you gave us the gift card, and we've used it to decorate our living room with great prints, vases and the most amazing marble coasters. Thanks for allowing us to share a little bit of your great style sense!

Love,
Frank and Kim

When Guests Can't Attend, But Send a Gift Card Anyway

You'll also find that many guests who love you but can't attend the shower (or the wedding itself) often send you a gift anyway. Sometimes they'll order a gift off your registry and have it shipped to you, and sometimes they'll send you a gift card. Why is a gift card the item of choice? Because guests can tuck it into a pretty greeting card of their choosing (not a printed message on an online order chart), and the postage is easy to manage. That adds up to a top choice for thoughtful givers.

Your thank-you note, then, will acknowledge their kindness and generosity without saying "you shouldn't have!" That's considered an ungracious comment, actually, so it's falling out of favor. Your thanks will be pure when you tell them first that you missed seeing them at the event, that everyone was asking for them and *then* what you selected as your gift with the card, or how you're using the gift they sent. It's always about the people first, then the material things . . . especially when someone thought enough to send you a gift without attending the party.

Dear Charla and Devon,

We missed you at the party! We hope you're feeling better, Charla, and we thank you so much for sending the great mirror set! It was fabulously thoughtful of you, and we are so grateful to have such amazing friends. ☺ We'll call soon to plan a night out, and drinks are on us!

Love,
Nancy and Bill

Dear Aunt Jill and Uncle Matt,

What a wonderful surprise to get your package! Thank you so much for the gift card and flower vase. The vase already has white roses in it and is on our kitchen windowsill, and we've used the gift card to complete our towels set! We send our love across the miles to you, we miss you and we'll have to make a plan to come out to Arizona for a visit sometime in the near future. Everyone sends their love to you! Especially us!

Love,
Sue and Keith

CHAPTER 7

Wrapped Wedding Gifts

There's an interesting phenomenon when it comes to wrapped gifts that will give you a slight challenge when you're writing your thank-you notes. As you may already know, in certain regions of the country, families and heritages, there's an understood rule about whether or not it's *okay* to give a wrapped gift. For some groups, you bring an envelope with money or a check instead. Wrapped gifts are just not done. Yet, there will be guests who don't subscribe to the cash-only rule. It's *their* regional, family or heritage practice to give a wrapped present . . . and in greater numbers, guests may not bring the gift to the wedding itself. In an effort to save you from lugging big boxes home after the reception, they may mail their gift to you before *or after* the wedding.

So that means you may have a blank on your gifts list next to their name when you return from the honeymoon and set up to write thank-you notes. Some wrapped gifts may not have arrived yet. Granted, this will be a minority of cases, but if it happens, don't panic. Know that some gifts do arrive a week after the wedding, if not later. Just be prepared to send your thank-you note when the gift *does* show up.

The New Rules for Wrapped Wedding Gifts

It's all about the details. Especially since you may have registered for these items, and the giver knows they were your choices, your gracious thank-you notes go beyond any simple thank you for an *item*. The key to writing a great thank-you note for a wrapped gift is sharing what you like best about the item. The sheets are incredibly soft. The china makes your dinner table look like a professionally designed magazine ad. You were thrilled to see that the kitchen mixer had a special set of tools for making bread dough, and now your house smells like banana nut bread. It was a perk you hadn't expected. Go for the details, like the intricate laser-cut design on those wineglasses and how many people have already complimented them.

If the gift gives life to something you already own, include that! Guests *love* when they can regenerate a favorite family heirloom or cherished home item with their gift. It's a wonder to them that they happened to choose the exact same delft blue–color vases that now allow you to bring your grandmother's china pattern out of storage. Their gift, even a modest gift of $20 shiny blue bud vases from Bed Bath & Beyond, just brought your grandmother's china from the attic to proudly put on display in your home. Especially if it's your grandmother's sister who was the giver, your thank-you note becomes priceless.

If your wedding date has not yet arrived, don't fear revealing that you're already using the gifts. Guests know that you'll rip right into these, and they can imagine your bliss at arranging your own kitchen or living room just the way you want it.

If you did a Happy Dance when you unwrapped that espresso maker, let the giver know that. It always brings a smile to the giver's face when he or she can just imagine you dancing around, holding their gift up in the air, and sounding like a breathless teenager gushing about all of the plans you have for after-dinner dessert parties where their gift will please your crowd.

Here is a big key, and I'll call it The Happy Dance Rule from this moment on. Some wrapped gifts are revealed with the guests present, such as at showers and some engagement parties. They saw the look on your face, they saw the joy you felt. But let's face it, you couldn't exactly jump up and do a Happy Dance in the moment because you had fifty more gifts to go and people were shifting in their seats, as is often the case at long bridal showers. Here is where you earn gold stars: Guests are *looking* for your reaction to their gift. And they know you can't do the Happy Dance right then. So share it with them later. "Aunt Margaret, I had to let you know that I was literally jumping for joy when I got home and unwrapped that fondue pot. I loved seeing it at the shower, but I'm *loving* unwrapping all the little dipping dishes and tasting the sauces. Rob and I love the colored finials on the ends of the dipping sticks. You should have seen us searching the freezer for some kind of meat to have our first fondue with!" Now *that* is allowing the guest to share the moment with you. It's the Happy Dance Rule. Guests positively *beam* when they get a note with so much detail and so much joy in your voice, visuals about your experience with it.

Speaking of visuals, keep the five senses in mind. You'll add a depth of experience to your wrapped gift thank-you notes when you discuss how the item *feels*, *looks*, *smells*, *touches* or *sounds* (such as music CDs or wind chimes). The better you are at conveying details with sensory enjoyment in mind, the more depth to your thank-you note, and—this is important—the more of a gift you give in return to your loved one.

Another key element to thank-you notes for wrapped gifts is complimenting the actual wrapping. Sure, some people just throw the decanters into a bridal-themed gift bag and shove in some tissue paper, but some people make gift-wrapping an art. They set aside time to find just the right wrapping paper, crimp the edges and attach a gorgeous tulle bow with iridescent ribbon. Perhaps they'll add a silver snowflake ornament as an accent to the box as well as a contribution to your holiday décor collection. You can tell they put some effort in, and it's a spotlight on *your* ability to appreciate their hard work. I've known people who showed well-written thank-you notes to their friends: "Can you believe they thanked me for how it was *wrapped*? They're such good people!" Something to keep in mind.

Here are some examples of wrapped-gift thank-you notes that illustrate the keys we've just discussed:

Dear Aunt Vanessa and Uncle Craig,

Thank you for the exquisite crystal decanter! It's even more beautiful than when we saw it in the store. With the heart details and etchings, it catches the light and makes our whole table shine! We absolutely love it and we thank you for giving us such a beautiful present. We loved seeing you at the wedding, and we'll be in touch to invite you to dinner at our new place.

With our love,
April and Ken

Dear Aunt Marissa,

It was so wonderful to see you at the wedding after so long! Living in Florida agrees with you—you look fantastic! Thank you so much for the serving set—our china pattern is now complete, thanks to you! You've given us something very special that we'll use forever, and someday hand down to our kids and grandkids (and no, we have no big announcement right now! ☺). We'll be headed to Amelia Island in August and we hope that we can arrange to see you while we're in the area. We'll be in touch!

Love,
Amie and Jackson

Dear Carla and Bob,

Where did you find the gorgeous leather throw pillows?! We're always amazed at your talent for finding the perfect, stylish gift from your world travels, and we love that you thought of us during your trip to South Africa! The stitching on the pillows is just phenomenal, and they have given a whole new dimension to our plain ol' brown couch. You really should have your own home décor show! These pillows are just amazing. Thank you! We're so happy to have spent time with you at the wedding, and we'll look forward to seeing you in June at Cindy's graduation!

Love,
Penelope and Aaron

Mention Your Honeymoon!

Your thank-you note for wedding gifts can include a mention of your honeymoon! Let your guests know that you're home, that you had an amazing adventure in an exotic location and now you're in the thrill of opening your wedding presents. The giver has extended the celebration for you with his or her gift waiting to be unwrapped. Even coming home to a great gift is an adventure for you! Share your joy...

Dear Misty, Bob and Lisa,

We're back! Our honeymoon was just a dream come true! Rainbows over the ocean, swimming with dolphins, massages on the beach . . . we can definitely get used to that! And even better was opening your gift as soon as we got home. Thank you! We love the wall sconces and we've already set them up above our fireplace—they add such a warm glow to our living room, and they remind us of the great lighting in the resort's restaurant! So you've given us a little of that mood lighting here in our own home! We're just thrilled to have them, and we send you big hugs across the miles for your very thoughtful (and very romantic) gift! Great to see you at the wedding, and we'll hope to see you again very soon!

Love,
Tracy and Derek

CHAPTER 8

Cash Wedding Gifts

If you're among the large percentage of couples whose families and friends traditionally give cash and checks as wedding gifts, you'll answer such kindness with a new style of thank-you note that's evolved for today's weddings.

A thank-you note for a monetary present goes beyond the past pale cliché of "thank you for your generous gift." That saying is gone as more couples find it to be blank and hollow, lacking in any real gratitude at all—as if they expected to be showered with cash at their wedding, and they'll dole out the one ho-hum compliment that the giver was "generous." Yes, we know that. But what *else* do you feel?

Avoiding "Cash Register Syndrome"

Before we get into the wording examples, I wanted to remind you of an important rule: There's no need to mention the exact dollar amount of each gift in your note. Doing so can come off like a receipt, much like a letter you'd get in the mail after sending in your donation to a charity or political party (as in, *"Thank you for your generous gift of $100."*) It tends to sound *less* personal and puts the emphasis on the wrong thing: the dollar figure. Instead, treat all monetary gifts the same, whether it's a $25 savings bond from your great-uncle on a fixed income or $500 from your godparents. The dollar amount means nothing in a thank-you note; it's your gratitude for the gift that means all. And what that gift will help create for your future. *That* is what makes guests feel special . . . their cash or check successfully helps you create your life after the wedding.

The Secret Trick for Showing Emotion in Your "Thanks for the Cash" Notes

Avoid the rubber-stamp thank you of the past with a true expression of your feelings and what the gift will allow the two of you to accomplish. Those who give cash as wedding gifts do so with an intention to support your future, and they may dig deep to give you a generous amount, particularly when money may be tight for them. So it's the ultimate form of consideration when you express true emotion in your note. Can't summon up words for your emotions? Here's a little secret trick: What would you say to their face if they walked up to you with three hundred dollars cash? You'd hug them, of course, and you'd thank them with emotion and excitement and joy. That's the key to writing thank-you notes for cash gifts—you have to express emotion, both for their generosity and for the dream their gift makes possible for you.

It's a tricky thing to thank someone for cash. Go too far, and you appear cash-hungry. Go too subtle, and you appear flippant about a generous present. The only way you can tell what's right for your situation, for each giver, is to speak it out loud in private and see how it feels. Imagine *you're* the giver of that amount to another wedding couple. What would you love to hear in return? (And for the record, "You shouldn't have!" is not a compliment, so skip that.) Try "This gift allows us to . . ." or "We're overwhelmed at your gift *because* . . ." to get you thinking. Write down the expressions that you speak and use those to build your emotion-filled thank-you notes.

Keep in mind, this "Say it out loud" trick isn't just for cash gifts. It works equally well for *all* of your wedding gifts and favors of time and support. I've included it here to spotlight the "capturing of emotion" need that's central to fabulous thank-you notes. Remember, it's the feeling, not the amount of cash or the value of that china set, that counts the most.

The New Rules for Cash Gifts

We've established that thank-you notes for cash gifts are not cliché and that they should be filled with excitement and emotion. You now have some new tools for how to accomplish this in your writing. But let's go further into the dos and don'ts of thanking for cash.

After you open the note with your expression of happiness, you'll get right into the functional aspect of the gift. The giver would love to know how he or she contributed to your dreams. So let them know exactly what their cash gift will accomplish for you, such as helping you with the down payment for a new home, covering the tuition for graduate school, setting up your home office, completing your china pattern, buying a new kitchen set, adding an addition to your home, creating a backyard terrace with a garden and so on. Give them a visual of what they've just made possible for your future life and lifestyle together.

There is a category that's out of bounds, though, and many couples find themselves in this bind. If you'll use the cash to pay off your credit card debt, that's not as impressive a revelation as your buying your dream home or going back to school. In today's new rules, this one should not be revealed. People don't get the same warm, fuzzy feeling when they hear you've used their gift to shovel yourselves out of any kind of financial hole. Let's say you *do* plan to pay off your high-interest credit cards with all of your wedding money. What do you say to the giver of cash? You won't make up an admirable action or embellish the truth. You'll simply say "Your gift allows us to meet our goals so much sooner than we had planned." No one but you needs to know that your goals are to pay off Visa, MasterCard or Discover. There is one kind of debt that *does* qualify and *can* be mentioned in your note. If you'll use the cash to pay off college loans, you *can* share this tidbit. Your guest has given you the gift of financial freedom from a positive type of debt, a clean slate to start the future.

Avoid any sense of competition. Never even hint at how generous everyone else has been with a message of "We can't believe how generous the entire family is!" or a very crass "Your gift put us past the four-figure mark!" That's offensive on so many levels. Your thank-you note should focus on their gift alone, so avoid mentioning how happy you are to get a giant windfall from your three hundred wedding guests. That comes off as greed, not gratitude, and that's the opposite of what you're working to convey in your successful thank-you notes.

Again, you won't delineate between large-sum cash gifts and the lesser. Remember that guests often display their thank-you notes in their homes. Keep that in mind! You should never use a generic, one-sentence thank you for guests who gave what you consider to be a modest gift (such as $50 when it's your family's practice to give $100 for wedding couples) while praising higher-tax-bracket guests who gave you $300. Each gift is generous in its own right, and no distinction should ever be made between amounts when you word your notes.

There's no need to specify whether you found cash, a check or a savings bond in your notes. In fact, it's best if you avoid any mention of the *form* of their cash gift and simply discuss your gratitude for their generosity, their giving nature and other words that you'll find in the Thesaurus at the back of this book. This insight is indeed a subtle one, but guests do report that "Thanks for the check," while accurate to say, doesn't carry the same emotional weight as wording that focuses on the contribution as an intention.

You'll see in the following examples different ways to approach cash-gift thank-you nuances. You'll see a sense of humor in some, and you'll be able to feel the surprise and excitement in others. Now here's a little tip: Highlight or circle the words that stand out to you in these examples. *Astounded. Jaw-dropping. Semi-speechless.* And if it's true to you, there's always "Words can't express . . ." which often expresses just the right thing to the giver.

Dear Aunt Sylvia and Uncle Howard,

We can't thank you enough for your wedding gift! You've given us a tremendous edge as we set up our home office and get our business off the ground! We're so incredibly grateful to you for your support of our dreams! We loved seeing you at the wedding and wish we had more time to sit down and talk with you. But we'll be sure to invite you to dinner sometime soon, and we'll be so thrilled to show you our new office as well!

We love you very much!
Lila and Tony

Dear Paul and Elaine,

Thank you for your wedding gift! We wish we could say that we'll put it to our nest egg, but we're pretty sure you'd approve of the way we spent it . . . scuba diving in Belize! We'll e-mail over the pictures so that you can see just what you've given us . . . a memory we'll have forever. It truly was a once-in-a-lifetime experience, and we thank you for making it happen! Great fun seeing you at the wedding, and we'll have to get together soon!

Love,
Mike and Clara

Dear Max and Claudia,

You've made our jaws drop with your wedding gift! Thank you so much! We're about to close on our first home—our dream come true!—and you've helped make it happen. Words can't express how much it means to us! Of course, you'll have to be among our first guests, and we'll think of you when we sign on the dotted line next week. We're just so grateful, thrilled and excited to see what the future has in store for us. Thank you for being a part of our beginning at the wedding—it was great to spend time with you, and we'll see you soon! ☺

Love,
Edina and Warren

Dear Mom and Dad,

We're just floored at your generosity! Thank you so much for your gift . . . we didn't expect anything beyond the beautiful wedding you've made come true for us, and this gift has us overwhelmed and semi-speechless. We're blessed to have such wonderful parents . . . you're priceless to us! We'll drink a toast to you now and very soon with you, as we're just thrilled beyond belief that we can start our future with so many things that we thought we'd have to wait, hope and pray for over time. You've given us so much all these years, and our hearts are over-flowing with gratitude for who you are as well as what you've given us.

Love,
Mina and Peter

Cash Gifts from Before the Wedding

Some of your guests will give you cash as engagement gifts, and it's an amazing return to them when you let them know their present enabled you to do something wonderful for your Big Day. They've given you a piece of your wedding dream come true. Imagine the thrill a great-aunt gets when she opens your card and sees that her $25 gift, as much as she hated that she couldn't give more, was used to pay for your wedding license. It's the most important part of the day! You've just given her a smile, and some relief that her modest gift didn't fade in comparison to more generous relatives.

Dear Aunt Ruth,

    Thank you so much for your gift! We've used it to get our wedding license, so we thank you for making this step of our journey come true! We couldn't be happier about our upcoming wedding, especially because we'll be surrounded by our much-loved friends and family like you. Big hugs to you, and thank you again for always being so special to us!

Love,
Sara and Gary

CHAPTER 9

Specialty Wedding Gifts

The new world of wedding registries—including charitable registries, honeymoon registries, even home down-payment registries—has changed the face of wedding gifts forever. Now, your guests can give you an experience like that scuba diving expedition in Belize, or they can donate to your favorite cause in lieu of getting you a household item gift. If you have everything you could ever need, as some couples do, these registries allow you terrific alternatives to the blender and the coffeemaker. Your registry can "give a little back" to the world in the form of charity. It could give you a once-in-a-lifetime honeymoon experience you'll someday tell your kids about. Your gifts could be the foundation of your life together—literally—if you have a home down-payment registry through your bank.

So how do you say thank you to someone who gave you a percentage of your honeymoon suite or made a fine donation to the American

Heart Foundation? That's what we're covering in this chapter . . . advice for thank-you notes sent for the newest specialty gifts.

Charitable Donations

You've set up your registry through such sites as JustGive.org or IdoFoundation.org to feature your selections of most-favored charities. Your guests will click on your choices, read a little bit about what the charity does, even see a message from you on why this charity is dear to your heart. The guest can then make an online donation in any amount they wish, and you'll receive a notification that they gave. Your wedding, then, just helped a good-hearted charity.

When your wedding gift comes in this form, your thank-you note should reflect a slightly different kinds of thanks. You're showing gratitude not just on your own behalf but for the cause. You're also sharing what the organization means to you, and any past history you have with the group, as well as acknowledging that their gift "gives back" to the world.

You're thrilled that the occasion of your wedding brings about the best gift possible—helping others—and still, you're mentioning that you can't wait to see the giver again soon. They're valuable to you as a person, a friend or a relative, and not just a gift-giver. Look at the following examples to see how you might word your thank-you notes for charitable registry gifts.

Dear Sue and Mike,

We've just received word that you donated to the Leukemia and Lymphoma Society through our registry, and we thank you so, so, so much for giving to the cause. As you know, we've both done a lot of work for LLS, and we actually met at a Light the Night Walk three years ago! So it means the world to us that we can give back a little bit to the organization and be a part of all the great things they are doing. We thank you from the bottom of our hearts and send a lot of love your way! Your gift has made our day! We'll see you at the wedding!

Love,
Yvonne and Michael

Dear Lisa and George,

Thank you so much for your wedding gift! We've just received word that you gave to the Susan G. Komen Foundation, which as you know means so much to us since Katie's illness. We're so thrilled that the blessings of our engagement are giving to so many others as well. Thanks for being a part of it! We're so lucky to have such wonderful friends like you! We'll see you on the wedding weekend—get ready for the softball tournament!

Our love,
Monica and Matt

Honeymoon Registries

Thanking a guest for a contribution to your honeymoon can be a tremendously fun thank-you note to write. You're sharing colorful details about the *experience* the giver made possible for you. Be sure to include senses in your note, such as how things looked, how they felt, how they smelled or tasted. You'll be using true writer's talent when you share your story in a way that lets the reader almost experience it as well!

One note, though: Since many honeymoon registry options include *shares* of pricier things like your airfare, your honeymoon suite, tours and spa treatments, you'll never thank anyone "for your share of" anything. They made your hotel room possible, and they made your airfare possible, so you'll thank them for the entirety of the choice. That's the number-one rule for these new registries.

Dear Shepard and Delilah,

We couldn't wait to thank you for your wedding gift! The helicopter tour you gave us was AMAZING! We spent an hour in the sky above Hawaii and saw unbelievable cliffs and waterfalls, all the colors of the rainforest, rainbows over the island and the ocean was so clear that we saw dolphins and even whales in the water! We were just speechless with how beautiful it was! We took fabulous pictures and will share them with you online! It was a dream vacation, and your gift gave us unforgettable views and memories to last a lifetime. Probably several lifetimes! It was great to see you at the wedding, and have a great time on your trip to Spain! We love you, and thank you again for such a fantastic and dreamy wedding gift!

Love,
Arline and Bobby

Dear Carole and Jeff,

We're back from Bermuda! Thank you so much for your gift! We had an amazing time, and we have to thank you for making that honeymoon suite possible! How terrific to wake up to the sounds of the ocean, and we had phenomenal breakfasts on our terrace overlooking the water. We're so grateful for the experience! Thank you!

We loved seeing you at the wedding, and we'll see you soon—

Love,
Deanne and Carlos

Dear Kelli and Todd,

We love you so much! Thank you for giving us the spa treatments during our honeymoon! We sooo needed them after the wedding, you wouldn't believe. The massage tables were set up right at the ocean's edge at sunset, and they started us off with champagne and mangoes. They painted us with avocado and massaged us with the softest sponges ever. It was the royal treatment, and we loved it! So thank you for making that possible. It was the best way to start our honeymoon. We loved seeing you at the wedding—Kailey's getting so big!—and we'll see you soon at the family reunion. Can't wait!

Our love to you,
Marissa and Ryan

Destination Weddings

Another new breed of thank-you notes has grown from the rising trend of destination weddings. When you plan your celebration as an island getaway for your group of family and friends, your thank-you note will go beyond the gift they gave you to an even more important gift . . . their presence at your Big Day.

While some engaged couples do pay for their guests' travel and lodging, not all do. So you'll thank them for the investment they made to be with you. That airline ticket may have been quite expensive, even with your group discount, and the guests may have made some cuts in their family budgets in order to attend. That deserves a tremendous thank you! And many couples do so by giving their destination wedding guests extra-special welcome baskets in their hotel rooms (see chapter 27), very exciting activities and tours during their stay at the resort, room upgrades, bottles of champagne upon arrival, even surprise limousine rides to the hotel.

Even after all that, your thank-you note after the wedding will express just how happy you were to have them there. You appreciate whatever sacrifices they made to make their flight, including overcoming airline travel uneasiness. *But,* you'll do so very subtly. You're thanking them for making the event extra-special without saying "We're so glad you spent $1,000 on airfare and lodging for us!" While you are, in effect, thanking them for their investment of time and money, your focus is on the gift of sharing the experience with them.

Dear Marjorie, Tom and Alinda,

Thank you for making our wedding weekend so amazing! We loved having you there and are just thrilled at how much fun everything was. Alinda, those were the best sandcastles we've ever seen! And thank you also for the gift of the Jet-Ski rentals for our honeymoon—we had a blast and have great pictures to share with you when we see you next.

All our love,
Nancy and Dan

Dear Allen and Renata,

We are so happy that we got to spend our wedding weekend with you! We know that it's your busy season, and we were thrilled when you said you were going to be able to make it! It wouldn't have been half as much fun without you! Thanks, too, for the wedding gift—we had a terrific time at the restaurant and clinked glasses in a toast to you.

Our love,
Diana and John

CHAPTER 10

The Groom Says Thank You for Gifts to Him

Grooms, you're trailblazers! This is the first decade where the men are—in large majority—full planning partners in putting the wedding together. This is your day, too. So it stands to reason that *you'll* be on the receiving end of gifts and service, help and favors from others as you work on your portion of the wedding plans. That means that some thank-you notes are yours to write.

No Excuses

While many men say, "I'm not good at etiquette," or "She does the note-writing," more and more men take the plunge and send out notes of their own. Why the big change in men writing thank-you notes now? It's partly gender equality and also partly just good character. You'll fire off a quick thank-you message at work when someone really comes through for you, right? Well, why not for your wedding, too? Yes, you may be your bride's tag-team partner in writing the wedding thank-you notes, but some messages will come purely from you as an individual. You'll impress the recipient with your class, your expression and your quick response.

In this section, I've provided advice on how today's groom expresses thanks, as well as examples of how you might word your own personal thank-you notes, from the simple to the detailed, the formal to the funny. Choose your style and see how you'd like to thank others for their gifts, and for networking on your behalf, helping you find that great gift for your bride, suggesting a location or honeymoon resort, flying in for your bachelor party or even helping set up surprises for your bride and her family.

Tips for the Groom's Notes

Find the format that's most comfortable for you. Are you more at ease with handwritten notes, or do you prefer to design your thank-you notes on the computer? Some grooms say they're not exactly proud of their handwriting, so they're not comfortable penning the actual notes. And this insight applies to brides as well! If handwriting isn't your forte, then you're free to design your own notes on your computer, use spell-check for backup, and then print the message out for you to *hand-sign*. That's always very important and one of the key etiquette rules for thank-you notes today.

Be specific about what you're expressing gratitude for, and include your bride in the note just as she includes you in notes that she writes. And use your sense of humor! You'll feel most comfortable writing notes that sound like you, which makes the task all the more enjoyable and makes sense to the recipient. Think about it . . . what would you think if you received a note from your buddy that didn't sound *at all* like him? He never uses the word *elegant*, perhaps. You'd probably think that the bride wrote the note, or that he copied it off the Internet and then just signed his name. Either you'd be amused or not at all impressed. That's not the goal of your notes.

Use that "speak it aloud" method you read about earlier, imagining yourself thanking the giver or the helper in person and then writing down exactly what you said. Wouldn't you talk differently to your college friends than you would to your grandfather, or to your boss? Use the "speak it aloud" trick to write down how you'd most comfortably thank these individuals in person. Sound like yourself, keep it brief and mention any future plans you may have with the recipient, even if it's just seeing them at the wedding.

Check out the following examples for how you can work your voice, your sense of humor, things you may have discussed with the recipient earlier, and of course the details of what you're thanking the recipient for.

Dear Greg,

    Just wanted to thank you for your help in tracking down all the guys' e-mail addresses and for covering the bases in getting their size cards going. Your help means a lot to me as Jen and I dig into all these wedding plans. I promise . . . we won't have you in pink ties.

Talk to you soon,
Mike

Frank,

Thanks for hooking me up with your tech guy for our wedding website. He really knows what he's doing, and it's making everything a lot easier on us. You've helped us save a lot of time, so that means I'll be available for those Wednesday tee times. You've saved my life and probably my sanity, too.

Thanks, buddy.
Ed

Dear Uncle Todd and Aunt Stephanie,

Thank you so much for letting Kari and I use your beach house for the wedding! I feel like I grew up there, and now that's going to be where we get married. It's just unreal. We thank you for your generosity and for how much it means to both of us to have the wedding in such an important place for all of us. We'll see you soon, with a bottle of wine in hand for you, and some gifts for the kids as well.

Love,
Craig

Dear Dad,

It means the world to me that you would give me your pocket watch to wear at the wedding. You really surprised me with that one, and I was so floored I didn't have the words right then to thank you. But I'm making up for it now. Thanks so much for that, and for being the kind of father that every man out there wishes he could have.

I'm very lucky.

Love,
Tom

CHAPTER 11

The Bride and Groom Say Thank You to Each Other

Of course, you'll smother your sweetheart with thanks in the form of hugs, kisses and other expressions of gratitude, but it's always a nice touch (and the best keepsake in the world) when you write a thank-you note to your intended. Today's brides and grooms list several key things that inspired them to write thank-you messages to one another. For instance, it may be a special gift, such as the night-before-the-wedding gift of bridal jewelry or a watch. This gift becomes a keepsake you'll hand down to future generations, and it's an added bonus when you can show the thank-you note as well. They also send thank yous for flowers sent throughout the planning process. (Some grooms are sending their brides surprise bouquets at work to take the edge off wedding planning stress, and that deserves a beautiful thank-you note in return.) Also on the list is support given during a tough time. For instance, if you know you've been cranky lately, extra stressed and snippy and your partner has been a saint in putting up with you, a great thank-you note shows the perfect level of gratitude for the unconditional love you're so lucky to share. Other great occasions for sending a heartfelt note of thanks: spontaneous getaways, day trips, perhaps even a pre-honeymoon or simply great work on the wedding plans, going above and beyond just to make you happy. For example, one couple in Minnesota wrote in about how the groom drove four hours to a terrific winery to pick up the cases of Pinot Noir the bride really wanted, as it was the vintage they were drinking on the night of their engagement. The winery wouldn't ship, so the groom took the ride with his buddies as a surprise to the bride. And of course, you can give a note just to say thank you for promising a happy life together, thank you for proposing marriage, thank you for accepting, thank you for embarking on this adventure together and so on.

Giving Notes to One Another

The fun in this category is not just the creation of your notes, such as handwritten messages on a napkin with a lipstick kiss or a computer-printed note, but in the presentation of them. You can slip the note into his or her briefcase for a surprise during the long morning commute, mail it during your business trip, leave it on a pillow or place it in the freezer next to the nightly ice cream treat.

There's no need to be formal with this category of thank-you note. Something fun and tailored to your personality is always appreciated. Are nicknames okay? Sure. These notes between the two of you are often for your eyes only, and couples say the regular surprises of thank-you notes keep the stress levels down between them when they feel appreciated and loved during this stressful time. So even if it's a bright orange Post-It on the bathroom mirror with a handwritten note from you, that works.

Remember, this category of thank-you notes opens the door for simple "I Love You" messages, with thanks for the life you're sharing, not just for gifts or favors.

Keeper Alert!

Hang on to these thank-you notes and all other love letters that you send one another before the wedding. They're marvelous keepsakes to look back on after the frenzy of the wedding time, and they'll serve as a fabulous reminder to you in the future of the blissful love you shared and expressed in the beginning. In the future, when inevitable clouds roll in to throw some shade on your partnership (only temporarily, of course), these thank-you notes bring you back. And they remind you to write more thank-you notes onward into the future for all the little thoughtful things that time would otherwise blur in your sight.

Dear Jennifer,

Thank you for saying Yes. Not a day goes by that I don't think about the look on your face when I proposed to you.

Love,
Brian

Dear Michelle,

Thank you for the watch. Finally, we upgrade my tired old 1980s version, and that's quite appropriate because look at the high-quality upgrade our life is about to take tomorrow. You've lifted me up to a higher level and you bring out the best in me. You're the best thing that ever happened to me, and I promise I'll spend each minute of my life making you as happy as I possibly can.

Love,
Jerry

My dearest, dearest Allen,

Thank you so much for the flowers! You make my day every day, and I'm so lucky to have you!

Love,
Leticia

CHAPTER 12

How to Say Thank You for Gifts You'll Return

It never fails. Someone, albeit with good intentions, ventures away from your registry and gives you a gift that you absolutely, positively, cannot use. Nor would you ever display it in your home. I've heard stories about cow-themed teapots, holographic red picture frames, Egyptian fertility dolls, scratchy blankets and Victorian lace bedspreads when your stated color and theme is a sophisticated, city-chic brown satin with indulgent throw pillows. The list of questionable bridal gifts goes on and on, and it's a "wince-moment" when you open that gorgeously wrapped box to reveal . . . something that's just not *you*.

Yes, you'll return it, no question about it. With no hard feelings. The guest was trying to please you, but missed the mark. Maybe those fertility dolls are quite valuable and the guest wanted to surprise you with the good-luck charms that she believes so strongly in. Maybe the guest with the cow-themed teapot confused you with a bovine-loving friend. Hey, accidents do happen.

Still, a thank-you note must be sent, and you can't come out and say, "What the heck were you *thinking*?!" You're now securely in the position of rising above and wording your thank-you note in the most diplomatic way possible.

Wording Your Notes Smartly

First, take a moment to remind yourself that the giver had good intentions. Believe it or not, if you're carrying an attitude of distaste, it *will* show through in your writing. Some people, albeit unintentionally, reveal a bitterness in the wording they choose. "It wasn't something we were expecting," or "We'll try to make it work with our décor" may be honest, but it can come off on the page like a literary slap in the face.

Instead, focus on the positive. As you'll see in the examples below, even a so-called bad gift can spring up an unexpected positive, like a memory of a family vacation, or something your great-grandmother owned. "I remember that my great-grandmother used to have a pickle plate just like this one!" You're being truthful, and the giver enjoys that the gift has sparked a cherished memory in you.

You don't need to be so honest as to explain that you'll be returning it, obviously. I include this tip here, even though it seems like a no-brainer, because I *have* heard from people who want to "teach the giver a lesson" to stick with the registry next time. Ouch! It's not your place to save all future relatives from Aunt Sally's penchant for pickle plates. It's bad etiquette to imply any message of disappointment, or one of correction.

Your best bet, then, is to thank the giver for thinking of you, and avoid ringing a false note with false praise. You can fill the space of your thank-you note with additional compliments, like how lovely she looked at the wedding, how wonderful it was to chat with her, how you're looking forward to seeing her again. You'll switch tracks to the personal angle of your thank-you note, complimenting the giver if not the gift itself.

Look at the following examples to see how the writer smoothes over the fact that the gift was not of their taste. They found a way to accentuate the positive in a *related* way, without being dishonest at all.

Dear Aunt Marie and Uncle Jim,

What an amazing gift! The lace bedspread reminds us of a vacation we once took to a lovely bed and breakfast in Cape May—so thank you for bringing back terrific memories of one of our favorite getaways. We may have to go back in the future, we loved it so much. Thank you for your thoughtful gift and for the additional gift it gave us in return. Lovely to see you at the shower, and we'll be seeing you soon at the wedding! Please give our love to all!

Love,
Marcia and Erik

Dear Julie and Jim,

How do you always manage to find such unique and amazing gifts? We've named our Egyptian fertility dolls Fred and Ethel, by the way! Very creative and thoughtful of you! Terrific to spend time with you at the shower, and we'll be seeing you soon!

Our love,
Rebecca and Ryan

It's clever without being the least misleading or dishonest, which is the challenge of writing a thank-you note in this situation.

Never, never, never lie. Never say it's the best gift you've ever received, just to avoid hurting someone's feelings, because in going too far to do something kind, you'll almost certainly set off alarm bells that something is very wrong. Too much gushing, too much complimenting, getting *way* too excited about a cow-themed teapot and you're naked with your false praise. After all, that cow-themed teapot could have been a joke gift because the DVD player they got you hasn't arrived yet. Be diplomatic always, find the silver lining, and thank them for the *qualities* they used in making their selection, even if it missed the mark. Your key words are *unique, creative, thoughtful, amazing, inspiring, lovely,* and *worldly.* My personal favorite is *stunning.*

It's Not Always Their Fault

You may have registered twice for something, or changed your *own* mind about something you added to your registry list. You may have bought yourself that bathroom accessory set and forgotten to take it off your registry, or the online store had a computer glitch and signed you on for four salad spinners.

This means you're the reason for the impending return.

Getting Their Help for a Return

When you need to request a gift receipt to return an item, be honest with the guest who gave it to you. Everyone knows how glitches may happen, and they'll respect your honesty. You can say that you hate admitting your own disorganization, but you registered twice for that salad spinner, and you know your friend will be willing to help you out with the gift receipt so that you can get the popcorn maker instead. A good friend or close relative will laugh with you and send you that gift receipt right away. You've humanized yourself, you can laugh at yourself and you show a beautiful sense of comfort with the relationship that you didn't fear asking him or her for the receipt. You may be returning their original choice, but you're fabulously grateful that they're now able to help you—just by sending you the little receipt—to get something else you can really use. And you'll send a thank-you note for that new item later.

Of course this works only when you've made the mistake, not when you changed your mind about your bathroom color theme. You can be honest that the color or texture is not what you expected, and would they please help you out with the gift exchange receipt? Who could say no to a request like that? (Plus, I'm told by many guests that they're often inspired by brides' and grooms' self-confidence in making the return . . . many people would feel hesitant to do so.)

Never fear . . . with the right wording, and with your own level of confidence and consideration for the giver's feelings, you can get that gift return receipt to make the change you most desire. And when you do it right, you'll leave no hurt feelings in your wake.

Where's the written note giving you the example? Ah, there is none. This request requires a phone call, so that the giver can hear the genuine feelings in your voice. If you have the chance, ask for it in person. Since this is a unique request, which—again—you're making because you're close to the giver, it's best to be more personable about it.

PART THREE

Thank You . . .
For Your Help

So many people have devoted their time, energy and enthusiasm to your wedding, and each playing their part, have made this a wonderful experience for you. Sending a thank-you note for their help, no matter how small their effort might seem, is perhaps the best kind of thank-you note they can receive! How gracious you are to take time out of your schedule to write out a quick message of gratitude! You're showing that you have your priorities in the right place, which makes you the best kind of wedding couple to work with.

I encourage you to send these little notes all the way through the process, and if you haven't yet, it's never too late to start! E-mails are fine for these (particularly if you choose cute, animated cards), as are quick notes written on your personal stationery or general boxed greeting cards with a great graphic on the cover (a starfish, butterfly, sunset, field of lavender, whatever you wish!). What matters most is that you take the time to say thank you for others' gifts of their time and generosity.

❖

CHAPTER 13

To Parents and Stepparents

Of all the "thank you for your help" notes, this category is perhaps the most important. Especially if parents and stepparents are generously helping to pay for your wedding, your repeated gratitude is definitely in order. Plus, there's an added benefit: Since tensions can run high as the wedding plans kick into high gear, either between you and the parents or amongst the parents themselves, consider your notes to be a healing balm that smoothes over growing resentments and stresses. A quick note of thanks from you, a reminder that you *do* appreciate all they're devoting to give you a great day, and all of a sudden that gnawing annoyance at the choice of appetizers doesn't even register with them.

And of course, even if there are no tensions, no bickering and everything's going swimmingly, that's even *more* of a reason to say thank you. You're among the lucky minority of couples who report a blissful partnering with parents. As one bride wrote to me recently, *"We knew our*

Soothing Words

The number-one cause of pre-wedding fights with parents is a feeling of being taken for granted or ignored, not being valued and generally (albeit sometimes fictionally) a feeling that you aren't appreciating all they're doing. Granted, the trouble may be theirs alone, but it never hurts to send an occasional thank you for all they're doing.

parents were a little bit bummed about our planning and paying for the wedding on our own, so we made sure we took extra care to thank them for the great job they were doing on the things we DID assign them. It made them very happy, and we felt better about it, too."

I've broken down the thank-you notes to parents and stepparents into three categories: Before, During and After, as you'll have different meanings and depths of sentiment in each.

Before

Right at the start of your wedding plans, one of the first major decisions you'll make is how involved your parents will be with the responsibilities, costs, time, effort and also the joys of working on your big event. This is a crucial decision that shapes the entirety of your planning process, as you're setting the foundation upon which you *all* will stand.

When parents offer their support, it's a gift of tremendous honor to you. The world is filled with countless couples whose parents withhold or retract their support, after all. It may be hard to imagine, but it does happen all too often. So when you invite them to participate in planning your wedding, in these days where more couples plan and pay for their own weddings, it's a tremendous honor for *them* that you wish to include them. Given the importance of these Moment One decisions, as you extend your hand to your parents and as they extend their generosity to you—no matter what the percentages of financial splits you all agree upon—you cannot start off the process with more heart and grace than thanking them for their offer or acceptance to help. Flowers, gifts and chocolates are fine for this task, but it's the words in your thank-you note that will stay with your parents far longer.

Your key goals with the "Before" thank-you note are to thank your parents for their offer to help, express your joy at the level of generosity they've offered (even if it's not the grandiose amount you expected or hoped for), and—most important—tell them how much you're looking forward to sharing the *experience* of working together. This is the time to mention anything special you can't wait for them to contribute, such as Dad's guitar playing, or Mom's superb singing. A big key: The "Before" thank-you note reveals that your *parents* have long been a part of your dream wedding plans. They may not have been aware of that. And this is one of the newest elements of a "Before" thank-you note.

Consider the examples below . . .

Dear Mom and Dad,

We can't thank you enough for your offer to pay for the wedding, and we're just beyond thrilled that we'll get to share in the excitement of planning with you. We know how lucky we are, as many of our friends didn't have the good fortune of planning with their parents, so we're looking forward to every minute. Now we get to add this to our collection of treasured family memories! We can't wait!

All our love,
Donna and Brian

Dear Mom and Dad,

We're so thrilled that we'll get to share the wedding plans with you. I've never told you this, but I always dreamed that both of you would walk me down the aisle and that Dad would play guitar with Uncle Augie at the reception. Now, finally, the dream is starting to take shape, and we both know how lucky we are to have our parents here with us, as excited as we are to begin. We love you, and we thank you so much for all you have offered to help us create our dream come true. This is going to be fun!

Love,
Angela and Barry

Are you "kissing up" to your parents for their big financial donation to your wedding? That's up to you. Again, the deepest intentions of your note will shine through in your wording. As you can see in the examples above, it's far better to mention how much it means to share the wedding planning *experience* rather than focusing on the blank check. This is the "Before" stage, after all, and keeping your priorities in line as you express your thanks will make the entire process go more smoothly. Parents feel appreciated, you feel grateful and blessed and you have started off in an admirable way.

During

Okay, this is where it starts to get interesting. Lots of decisions are being made, lots of opinions are flying around your heads. His mother wants a strawberry-filled cake and a church wedding, while her mother wants a chocolate cake and a garden wedding. Everyone has a financial stake in the wedding plans, and Cousin Charla's innocent phone call about a delay in shoe dye orders has pushed everyone over the edge. It's no secret that emotions flare and people get edgy during the wedding-planning process. Here's where the "During" thank-you note comes into day-saving play.

You can return everyone to their senses and their right priorities by sending out heartfelt thank-you notes just before the proverbial pressure cooker starts bulging. When the plans start getting hectic and your family starts snapping, this "During" note can turn down the heat with a well-timed reminder that they *are* loved, they *are* appreciated, you *do* love them—even when you must stand up for the most important parts of your wedding day—and that you're still honored to share the plans with them. You might apologize if you've been a handful to deal with, and show humility, which puts everyone else at ease as well.

Even without any hassles or pressure cooker scenarios, the "During" thank-you note is well-earned by your loved ones for their maturity and respect for you. Everything is going well, you're all happy, the wedding day is approaching without drama . . . that should certainly be celebrated with a note. It's the couples who forget to say thank you in the "During" stage who court meltdowns and power struggles, those blowups that don't need to occur. Again, it's not kissing up. It's providing positive reinforcement as you head into the emotionally charged remaining weeks and days before your wedding. And it's just a nice thing to do. With all you have on your mind, and on your To Do list, you thought to sit down and write thank yous to your parents and stepparents. Nice.

As an added tip for this category: Include details. They'll love it when you mention you noticed the extra legwork that went into finding the new cake baker. They'll laugh when you remind them of just how bad those samples were at the first one. They may tear up when you share an observation you made that they weren't aware of—"I saw the look on your face at my dress fitting yesterday. I know I'll never forget that moment."

Dear Mom and Dad,

You've been terrific through the planning, and as things are getting busier and busier, we wanted to take a moment and thank you for all you've been doing to give us this great wedding day we have planned. We thank you for your generosity, your excitement, and your very great ideas, and we'll always remember how much better this entire process was because you've been so wonderful about everything. We're incredibly blessed and words can't really capture how grateful we are for you.

Love,
Anna and Tomasso

After

No matter how the process went—everyone got along smoothly with no fights or power struggles, or even if someone behaved regrettably (blame the emotional charge that affects most wedding planning teams)—you're a gracious and well-bred couple to send thank-you notes to your parents for any part they played in your day. Think back past the whirlwind of your own tasks to really appreciate the thoughtful things they did, the investment of the money they devoted, the travel they undertook, the calls of comfort when you were having a hard time and the advice they gave you on having a happy marriage. Thank them for the special moments on the wedding day itself, such as how much it meant to you when you hugged your parents goodbye at the end of the reception, or the moment you shared when your mother affixed your veil. Now is the time for those revelations. It will be the best thank-you note your parents will ever have received in their lives. Anyone can say "Thanks for all you did." But when you add in *these* details after the wedding is over . . . that's priceless. And it's the essence of what makes the perfect thank-you note.

Dear Mom and Dad,

Thank you so much for giving us the wedding of our dreams! Actually, it SURPASSED our dreams and we can't thank you enough for everything you did to make it happen. It's a wonderful thing to share the compliments we've received from everyone, telling them that the Bentley was your surprise to us, that Dad made the chuppah, that Mom found the pianist for the cocktail hour.

We loved having so much of "you" in our day, and that made it all the more special to us. We can't thank you enough for the wedding you gave us, and for being such loving parents and great role models for the life we're building together now.

All our love,
Nancy and Vincent

When Parents Are Minimally Involved

The previous examples show you how to mix together thanks for parents' enormous and generous help with your wedding, as in the case when parents pay for all or most of the wedding and spend a *lot* of their time and effort in helping out. If yours is a case where you've decided to pay for your own wedding—a growing trend these days—then how do you thank your parents? They may have taken on only one or two small tasks, or they may have *wished* to take on more tasks but just weren't in a financial or health position to do so.

Your thanks will still be as full and genuine as they would be if your parents had paid the whole bill. You'll thank them for a lifetime of support and generosity, rather than focus on the year's worth of investment in your wedding. Focus on the sentimentality of their support rather than dollar signs. This is a chance for you to thank them for all they did

A Letter from Just You

When you're thanking parents for a lifetime of love and support, it's a wonderful idea for you as an individual to write your parents a letter describing what their love means to you. Some brides and grooms choose simple greeting cards that capture their sentiments perfectly, while others write ten-page letters on pretty stationery going into detail about what's on their minds right now. Parents cherish these kinds of thank-you notes, filled with memories and their words of wisdom that they didn't even know you remembered. It's the kind of letter that every parent dreams of receiving from an adult daughter or son as they face this big transition of your life (which is also a *big* transition in their lives). They'll keep it forever, so consider writing a note as an "I" in addition to the one you send as a "We."

to guide you through life to this point. That's your main focus. And then you'll thank them for their help, no matter to what degree, with the wedding.

Dear Mom and Dad,

Thank you for being such a special part of our wedding day. It meant the world to us that we could share this special time with you, to dance with you, laugh with you, and we'll always, always remember your toast to us. Everything you given us, now and in the past, from memories to lessons to celebrations, comfort, support and encouragement, means more than we could ever express.

With all our love,
Kim and Dennis

CHAPTER 14

To the Bridal Party

Your bridal party members have devoted their time, attention and perhaps a significant amount of money toward the goal of making you happy. They love you, and it's not a matter of "service" to you, but rather an honor they value (even if they have been cranky or difficult at times during the length of your engagement . . . everyone's allowed a bad day once in a while!). You'll certainly send them thank-you notes for the gifts they give you—whether it's an engagement, shower or wedding present—but these wonderful people will appreciate your thanks for the many tasks they help you with, or for the many ways they calm you, comfort you or share in your excitement. After all, these are busy people, with packed lives of their own, and they're taking what little time and energy they do have left over after work and family demands, busy social lives, school obligations and other hectic activities to do what you need them to do.

If you liked the idea of thanking your parents Before, During and After, you may certainly do the same for the members of your bridal party. The examples here are broken down into three main categories that you'll use to tailor your notes appropriately.

Thank Yous to Adults in Your Bridal Party

Before you begin writing your individual notes to your bridesmaids, groomsmen, maid of honor and best man, as well as any other honor attendant you appoint, take a moment and list for each person the three things they did during wedding planning that stood out. For instance, you might write down, *"Sarah established our Wednesday lunchtime manicure ritual, found the great shoe store and managed that little 'problem' with my sister."* When you write any "After" thank-you note, you'll have your details all laid out for you.

Of course, a quick note of thanks throughout the process, such as right after Sarah gave your sister the talking-to she needed, gives dear Sarah an instant smile. You're showing that you love her *now*, you see what she's doing on your behalf and you're not going to wait to let her know how much you appreciate her. It could be an e-mail or a quick note in the mail, even a memo left on her desk or on her front porch—all that matters is that you're saying thank you at the right moments to all of these friends and family who are taking time out of their busy lives to do for *you*.

As for who should sign these notes, you'll both sign them in your own handwriting when a favor has been done for your wedding as a whole. You're both the recipients of the favor when your adult attendants are serving your experience as a whole. But when a favor is for the bride personally, such as suggesting the perfect salon for the wedding morning, it wouldn't make sense for the groom to sign on. Check out the examples here to see how the signing rules look in real life:

Dear Marsha,

Just a quick note to say thank you for all you're doing to help me out with the wedding plans! You've been so terrific with everything, and you're making it possible for me to enjoy this whole planning process in the midst of all the craziness! I did the right thing when I asked you to be my maid of honor! So thank you, and martinis are on me the next time we go out . . .

Love,
Ariel

Dear Brandi,

You made our day! Thank you so much for recommending Carlos at White Star Bakery. You're right . . . he is just terrific, and we can hardly believe the artistry of his wedding cakes. You made our decision easy, and we wanted to thank you for helping us with this very special task. Big hugs to you!

Love,
Jen and Russell

Dear Jeff,

Thanks so much for your great work on the guys' tux shopping trip. It's not easy to keep those guys in line, but you make it look easy. We both appreciate all you're doing! There's a toast coming your way at the wedding, and we have a single bridesmaid for you, too. ☺

Leslie and Jim

Dear Evan,

Thanks for the words of encouragement, man. I owe you one.

Arnie

Dear Josh,

Thanks for offering to make the CD mixes for us! We know you're busy, and we appreciate the time and effort you're putting into creating our playlists. And thank you for hunting down that original recording of our song. When we got that message from you, it was the best news ever. You made one of our top wishes come true. So, thanks to you, our first dance will be even better. You're the best!

Love,
Tara and Keith

> Dear Adele,
>
> As always, you give the perfect advice. ☺ Thank you from the bottom of my heart.
>
> Love,
> Nicole

Thank Yous to the Children in the Bridal Party

Whether or not kids behaved themselves at the wedding, they get a thank you as well, and it's also good form to send a little note after any special shopping trips during the process, such as hunting for their wedding day wardrobes. Some brides take the kids out for pizza or ice cream after these excursions, but it's also a sweet gesture for you to send that note. Again, the more detail you can include in your note, the better. The kids will therefore learn just what they did well, which makes for a great life lesson in this unforgettable experience for them.

> Dear Anna and Elise,
>
> Thank you for being the best flower girls ever! You did a fabulous job with the rose petals and everyone said you looked so pretty in your dresses and wings! We loved dancing with you, too!
>
> Big hugs to our little angels—
> Aunt Shauna and Uncle Bill

Dear Hannah,

Thank you for being such a wonderful junior bridesmaid! Aunt Lisa said you helped out so much with the shower, and that you made all the favors yourself! You're such a great artist! Everyone loved the journals you made, and I'm using mine to record all of my memories as the wedding gets closer. I'll keep it forever, and I'll always remember that it came from you.

Love always,
Aunt Laura

Dear Devon and Daniel,

You were the most handsome ring bearers ever! So smooth! Great job during the ceremony, guys! To thank you for being so great at the wedding, we got you both a little something special. We hope you have a GREAT time at the game!

Love,
Aunt Sarah and Uncle Mike

Thank-You Notes to the Parents of the Child Attendants

As mentioned earlier, the parents did their fair share of work and may have kicked in a significant amount of money for the kids' outfits, party gifts and more. Many brides and grooms make the mistake of forgetting the parents' efforts, so be sure to add these helpful loved ones to your thank-you-note list . . . even if they themselves were in your bridal party. Get those details in there: the little things you noticed, like when they replaced the light purple sashes with the deeper purple you really wanted—and they did it without complaint. And if their kids were well-behaved, you can pay them no better compliment.

Dear Carolyn and Peter,

Thank you so much for all of your terrific efforts in getting the girls ready for the wedding. We LOVE the dresses and we thank you so much for the work you did on their sashes and hats. They're going to look so adorable on the wedding day! Nancy tells us that you were a dream to work with on the shower, and that the girls had a lot of fun making the cupcakes, so we just wanted to express our deep gratitude for all you've done to help us out. We love you all very much! See you at the wedding!

Love,
Kendra and Alex

Dear Marielle and Thomas,

The boys did such a great job at the wedding! And we wanted to thank you for making it possible for them to be such a wonderful part of our wedding. We appreciate everything you did, and where did you find that tux for the baby? Adorable! Pictures will be on the way soon, and again . . . thank you.

Love,
Helen and Gerry

CHAPTER 15

To Those Who Helped with the Wedding

While not everyone who helped out with the wedding was a member of the bridal party, they still came through for you. Perhaps you asked them to do a reading during the ceremony or hand out the programs. Perhaps out of the goodness of their hearts, they allowed you to use their home, their car, their business contacts, their private club as the location for your rehearsal dinner, their yacht, their computer, scanner and printer. Perhaps they offered to make your wedding cake or your groom's cake, or to perform a musical number at your ceremony or reception. Whatever they did to help, your thanks can be expressed in writing and in gift form. (See chapter 26 for ideas on gifts for these folks who are generous in time, money and spirit.)

The Keys to Great Notes for Helpers

If anyone deserves a thank-you note, it's these kindhearted people who stepped in *without* any expectation or obligation as a part of your bridal party or as a parent. So your key to writing great thank-you notes for these people is to *acknowledge that*. They didn't have to help, *they wanted to*. And that's what means the most to you. So you'll reflect your appreciation with that in mind and in word, bringing to the forefront the details you noticed about the tasks they performed.

How did they go above and beyond the call of duty? You noticed it, so share it with them. What exactly about their contribution did you love? What stood out? How did they astound you with their delivery? Tell them how it felt to get that call with their offer to use their home, and share any compliments you heard *others* say about their contribution. Your note not only thanks, it praises.

Tell them what it meant to you to have them play a role in your wedding. Your day was all the more special because *they* added something special. You asked them to be in your day for a reason. Given the fact that many people still help out even after you couldn't allow them into the bridal party for space reasons, a great thank-you note shows that you love them just the same.

Another element of a great thank-you note for helpful people: referring to past memories. Since the theme is the generosity of their hearts, you bring your point to a beautiful spotlight when you go beyond what they did for you now to acknowledge what they did for you back *then*. For instance, you might refer to the work they contributed to moving you into your new home, or how they've always made the family parties special with their gourmet cooking. When you thank them for their *legacy* of helpful works, you honor them in the most meaningful way.

As you'll see in some of the examples of this chapter, you might wish to give a gift in addition to the thank-you note. A charm bracelet, flowers, perhaps the same gift you chose for your bridal party and other suggestions in chapter 26, all are open for the giving.

One word of warning, though: *Never* say, "We should have had you in the bridal party!" Yes, you mean it as a compliment, but that's a statement that has put a sour taste in some helpers' minds. I've heard from some kind helpers who didn't quite appreciate the reminder that they weren't chosen for the bridal party. It had hurt them at first, but they overcame the perceived slight and rose up to contribute wonderfully to your day, because that's what their character is. Somehow, hearing, "You should have made our cut" delivers the wrong message and misses the mark on what should be a purely appreciative letter with no reference to the bridal party. So, obviously, saying, "You did so much more than our bridesmaids" or any other comparative statement is just not advisable.

Look at the examples here to capture the right tone and perhaps "borrow" the wording for your own thank-you notes in this category:

Dear Denise,

Thank you so much for the wonderful job you did with the reading at our ceremony. It meant so much for us to include you, as the person who introduced us to one another, in such an important part of our celebration. We hope you enjoy these flowers as a token of our appreciation, and we thank you for giving such life to the words that really were the foundation of our wedding ceremony.

All our love,
Charlie and Roxanne

Dear Leticia and Stanley,

Thank you! We heard from everyone that your greetings at the church entryway really set the stage for our wedding! We hear you were quick on your feet when the whole parking issue came up, and we so appreciate your efforts to fix the problem with us being none the wiser about it. Thank you for saving the day and starting off our day with the warmth of your friendly smiles that we love so much. We're so grateful that you offered to be our greeters, and we'd like to take you to dinner as a gesture of our thanks. We'll see you soon!

Love,
Carmen and Bryan

Dear Garrett,

Thanks so much for letting us use all of your computer ink! You saved us a bundle, and it was so much fun working on our invitations at your place with you. That was the best chili we've ever had, too! We hope you enjoy this gift card to Williams-Sonoma with our thanks and big applause to you for always being there for us, always being helpful and never laughing at what computer know-nothings we are! We'll see you soon, and thanks again!

Love,
Michael and Celeste

Dear Melanie and Brad,

We can't thank you enough for opening your home as the perfect setting for our wedding! We remember attending a backyard party at your place years ago, and our conversation in the car going home was the first time we ever talked about getting married in the future. All because your garden is so beautiful, we thought we'd love to get married there someday! And now our wish has come true! Thanks to you, we had our wedding in our dream setting, and everything was just so beautiful and exotic for our day. The kids LOVED the koi pond, too! So thank you from the bottom of our hearts, hug your landscaper for us and we hope you enjoy this case of wine as our thank you. We'll hug you when we see you again very soon.

Love,
Aimee and John

CHAPTER 16

To Your Wedding Coordinator

If you've hired a wedding coordinator to handle all or even part of your wedding plans, you know that you couldn't have done it without her. She's worked magic with your plans, revealed hidden gems of locations, spent all night ironing tablecloths for your guest tables and basically took on the pressures and the stress of your wedding plans so that you didn't have to.

So many couples refer to their coordinators as a guardian angel or fairy godmother of sorts, the person who miraculously took their descriptions, ideas and dreams and turned them into reality. Wedding coordinators steer you clear of potential problems and pitfalls and save you money with smart and stylish alternatives. Your coordinator may even have smoothed over conflicts with your parents or with bridal party members, expertly eliminating blowups and grudges with a simple diplomatic message and a hug. The complete image and experience of your day evolved from the mastery, artistry, dedication and often friendliness and calming influence of the wedding coordinator.

The thousands of wedding coordinators that I have spoken to say they greatly appreciate hearing "Thank You!" Believe it or not, some egregiously ungracious couples consider these experts to be "just doing their jobs" and thus go no further than handing over a check at the close of the reception. They act like these coordinators, who have sweated the details for months and perhaps lost sleep over some of the challenges, are mere employees. *You, however, are not that kind of person.*

The overwhelming trend these days is to present your wedding coordinator with a gift, perhaps a bouquet of flowers or a vase filled with a floral arrangement, or a wonderful gift such as the ones mentioned in chapter 26. Brides and grooms tell me that since they've gotten to know their coordinator as a person, and he or she may become more like a friend during the process, they search for a gift that's more personalized.

Make Your Coordinator's Day with the Perfect Note

As for your thank-you note, know that most coordinators love these so much, they display them in their offices. Yes, the fringe benefit is that the note serves as a business tool to show prospective clients (it's just smart business), but imagine the thrill when a frenzied coordinator has spent an entire day fielding calls from angry, demanding brides and their parents, vendors who pull out of contracts not to mention their own personal lives' daily stresses . . . and then gets a beautiful thank-you note from you. It's priceless to them, as coordinators repeatedly tell me. Everyone likes to be thanked and validated for their hard work. These experts care about you personally, so it's a beautiful thing when you show that you care about them personally as well.

When writing your coordinator's thank-you note, look for that personal connection. For instance, Kelly and Carl from Massachusetts knew that their coordinator collected starfish as a personal hobby. So they went out and bought a sterling silver starfish paperweight and engraved it with a thank-you message from the two of them. It's this personal touch that brings joy to a coordinator, who is too often treated as a nonentity by other couples. You will make your planner's day.

As for creating a touching and rewarding thank-you note for your coordinator, the process is a little more involved. After all, you're writing to a professional *in* the wedding industry. What will matter most to him or to her is not so much the same "love and family" history depth that your other notes will have, but rather a revealing look at *what* you appreciated about the project that was your wedding.

So be specific about which tasks meant the most to you. Coordinators live for details, so they beam when you write about the beauty of the calla lilies and how they really were the perfect choice over white roses. Coordinators love it when your note mentions how happy you were with the entertainers, the menu and how much the coordinator respected your wishes for what you didn't want. Think back over the day and share your recollections. How did you feel when you walked into the sanctuary and saw your described setting come to life? What was the first thing you noticed in that big moment—the raining orchids suspended from the rafters? The candles? Which little details caught your eye?

What did you hear your guests complimenting? In the moment, you undoubtedly told them about your heaven-sent wedding coordinator and accepted the compliment on his or her behalf. Now, when it's time to say thank you, you'll share those comments with the pro who made your day truly spectacular.

Perhaps most important, express what she meant to you as a *person*. It's not just the lineup of tasks, the arrangement of candles or buffet items, or the expertly handled contracts that pleased you, but rather the joy of working with a *real* person who listened to you, valued your opinions, comforted you, stepped in as mediator. A few moments ago, I

Smile for Your Coordinator

One extra note: It's a wonderful idea if you enclose a copy of your wedding portrait with your thank-you note. Coordinators love receiving these pictures! It's you on your Big Day, smiling and radiant, reflecting not just your love of one another but the excitement of the day you've planned together. Consider it your "After" picture, which will be quite fun for the coordinator to see as visual proof of your joy.

shared with you the sad report that some coordinators are treated like nonentities by some brides and grooms, as if they were nothing more than paid servants. Focus well on avoiding this. Make some reference to how much you enjoyed working with the coordinator as a person, a friend. Sometimes, the coordinator is friendlier than sisters or bridesmaids or mothers. When it's the coordinator who made the process pleasant for you, that certainly adds a depth of heart to your thank-you note.

When you are ultra-pleased with the coordinator's work, mention that you'll recommend the coordinator to others. In their competitive field, they depend on referrals, and this is your chance to "give a little back." And don't be surprised if your thank-you note, for all of its spectacular detail and emotion, goes on display in the coordinator's office for both pride and value and also as a nice thing for future clients to see.

Check out the following samples for inspiration on the phrasing and details that are perfect for coordinators' thank-you notes:

Dear Elaine,

What a beautiful job you did with the wedding! It was absolutely a dream come true, and we have you to thank for bringing our every request to life. We're SO glad to have had you in our corner, guiding us so perfectly and allowing us to ENJOY the process. Everything was just beautiful and the food was amazing—you made it perfect, and we're so grateful to have had the blessing of working with you. We'll surely recommend you to everyone we know.

With our thanks and love,
Carmen and Hector Arroyo

Dear Delilah,

Hello from St. Lucia! We couldn't wait until we got home from our honeymoon to thank you for everything you did to help us plan the wedding of our dreams. You constantly amazed us with your ability to handle all of the details in rapid-fire pace, always keeping your cool even with that unfortunate florist situation! You kept our sanity in line as well, and allowed us the security of knowing that we were in good hands. You've become like a friend to us, and we'll be calling you when it's time for the baby shower! Thank you so much for all you've done for us . . . You're the best thing that could have happened to our wedding!

All the best,
Danielle and Michael Holloway

Don't Forget the Assistant and Staff!

In many coordinators' offices, it's the staff who does a lot of the heavy lifting, delivering your messages, replying to your emails and running errands, so be sure to thank them as well. Yes, the coordinator was in charge and did amazing things for you, but the assistants played their part as well. A separate card or gift for the staff is a wonderful idea. Wedding couples tell me they sent baskets of brownies or muffins to the staff at the office, or individual gifts such as charm bracelets, flower arrangements, even items from their supply of wedding favors.

Dear Andre,

We can't thank you enough for your guidance and genius in planning our wedding celebration. It was always a big sigh of relief on our part when we saw it was you on the phone, and your encouraging us to think big and make it personalized gave us a better, more meaningful wedding than we could ever have planned on our own. You're the best, and we're so grateful that we got to work with you, and that we got to know you. You're just one of those people who puts a smile on people's faces and makes the world a better place. Whenever we look at our wedding pictures, we'll think of you and how we wouldn't have had any of that without you! We wish you all the best, and again, you have our thanks and adoration.

Eve and Saul Jackson

Dear Sarah,

Thank you so much for everything you did to help us create our dream wedding day. We apologize for changing our minds on those table linens so often, and we thank you for always being so sweet whenever we called with yet another "tweak"! It was a joy to work with you all of these months, and we hope you enjoy these chocolate-covered strawberries as a token of our gratitude for all you did to keep us on track. We wish you well always, and we're so glad to have met you.

All the best,
Barbara and Jeff Kelly

CHAPTER 17

To Your
Wedding Experts

Just like with your wedding coordinator, your wedding experts—the florist, caterer, cake baker, photographer, videographer, entertainers, invitation designers, gown designers and others—all devoted their talents and their desire to please *you*. Don't think they're in their careers just to make money; their industries are competitive, grueling and challenging, and they thrive in their work because they truly care about making you happy. Each has guided you. Each has brought the best of what he or she is capable of because they know it's your wedding day.

When they please you, it's a mark of class and generosity when you take an extra step to thank them as well. It's up to you if you want to give a gift of gratitude, as you might for those experts who really went above and beyond what was expected of them, but the overall trend is for a heartfelt thank-you note that they'll appreciate and yes, perhaps display in their studios for prospective clients to see.

Top Tips for Wedding Expert Thank-You Notes

Just like with your wedding coordinator thank-you notes, the key to a great message to your caterer, florist and other masters of wedding creation is in the *details* you include. Be specific about what their task meant to you, what you loved the most about their work. Again, these experts are in the fields they're in because they're detail-oriented, perhaps perfectionists. They do care about the work they do for you, and they may have put in many, many hours bringing your wishes to life. They work hard to surpass your expectations. Your thank-you notes bring them a wonderful sense of validation when you say that you *noticed* the perfection of those chocolate curls on the cake, the exquisite taste of the passed hors d'oeuvres or the couldn't-have-been-better musical performances. So before you sit down to pen your wedding-expert thank yous, take some time together to list what stood out, where you felt the experts went above and beyond.

Again, share the joy of your guests' rave reviews, knowing that your experts were toiling on your behalf or left the premises as per their business practices, having missed out on all the compliments you heard. Include the best of them in your note, knowing you'll make the expert's day with a comment he may have been wishing he'd hear someday. Without you thinking of him, he'd walk away without ever knowing.

Just as with the wedding coordinator, of course, thank them for the pleasure it was to work with them as people, how their sparkling personalities made the process all the better, and offer to refer them to others, if you will. Sign with your last name, as many experts work with many couples over the course of the year; you may even wish to send the expert a picture of you enjoying their food, their cake, their flowers, and so on.

On the following pages, you'll find examples of the kinds of letters sent to a variety of wedding experts. Look for the details, the evidence of the tips offered here and use your own notes on what impressed you most in order to give greater depth and personality to your thank-you messages.

Your Florist

Dear Kathy,

The bouquets just took my breath away! Not fair making me cry right before the ceremony! Thank you so much for the beautiful job you and your team did on all of our flowers. The floral bracelets for the mothers were an especially big hit with our guests, and everyone complimented the cabernet calla lilies in the centerpieces. We had no idea that callas came in that color, so thank you for all of your amazing advice and expert creations. My biggest wish for my wedding was that it would be a sea of beautiful, breathtaking flowers, and you brought my wish to life! Thank you from the bottom of my heart—

All the best,
Shauna Ryerson-McKenna

Your Caterer

Dear Edgar and Carlos,

Your menu at the wedding was a work of art! Almost too beautiful to eat, but everything was just delectable. All of our guests raved about the food, and we can't thank you enough for your great suggestions, your dish pairings and advice on the food stations. Thanks to you, our celebration was a big success and you've set the bar high for other relatives getting married soon! We've already referred you to so many of our friends and family, and we do so with the highest gratitude to you. Here's wishing you all the best!

Our thanks,
Susan and Charlie Banks
Married at the Breakers, 5.27.06

Your Cake Baker

Dear Ron,

We almost fell over when we saw the beautiful cake in our reception hall! It's actually on our wedding video that I gasped when I saw it. What a work of art! No one could believe the flowers were pulled sugar paste and not real flowers, and more than a few of our guests called the cake "orgasmic." Not sure if you've received THAT kind of compliment before. ☺ We LOVED the cake and will love the top layer again on our first anniversary. Thank you for the time and effort you put into our wedding cake—we can tell how much passion you have for your art, and we're grateful to be among the lucky couples who get to have YOU design their cakes. We'll spread the word that you are the man to see!

Our thanks and applause for your wonderful work,
Sasha and Kyle Hendricks

Your Banquet Manager

Dear David,

You made everything wonderful for our wedding! We knew when we met you that this was going to be a fabulous experience and we were thrilled beyond our hopes with just how perfect our day was. Thank you for all of your hard work and attention to detail. You made us, and all of our guests, feel like royalty. We'll look forward to working with you and your terrific staff in the future for other special events, as there's no one else we'd rather have as our partner.

All the best,
Diane and Don Winters

Your Entertainers

Dear Phillipe,

We can't thank you enough for the beautiful music you played at our cocktail party. Every so often, we forgot it was a live performance and thought it was a professional recording! We thank you for your beautiful talent and your playlist. Each song made us smile with the wonderful memories it brought to us. It was just a delight to have you at our wedding.

Our best wishes for your certain success in the recording industry,
Daylle and Daniel Jenkins

Dear Michael Hanks and the Starlight Trio,

You really know how to keep the party going! We all had a blast at the wedding, thanks to your phenomenal performance! We thank you for the great show; our guests are still talking about the fabulous music and how packed the dance floor was all night! You made our celebration a rocking success and we thank you so much!

Felicia and Taylor Aaronson

Your Limousine Driver

Dear Seamus,

We wanted to send you a special thank you for chauffeuring us on our wedding day! Your sparkling wit and genuine congratulations made our ride to the ceremony quite memorable—you're one of those people who just brings about smiles and laughter, and we still talk about how funny you were! Thank you for making "our first ride" so special!

With all best wishes, and we'll see you again!

Melanie and Tony Oliveres

Your Invitations Specialist

Dear Georgia,

The invitations came out beautifully! Thank you for your extra-special attention with the fonts and the colors, and your design was just magnificent! We received so many compliments from our guests and have sent many of them to your website. Thank you for your inspiring artistic talent and for how quickly you sent everything! We adore you and thank you for all your efforts. We'll be displaying the invitation in our home along with our wedding picture—it's so gorgeous, it has to be shown off!

With all best wishes and our deepest gratitude,
Lila and Sam Taylor

Your Gown Designer or Sales Clerk

Dear Felicity,

You made my gown shopping excursion so perfect! I knew when I walked into your salon that I was "home!" Thank you so much for your help in choosing my dream dress, and for talking me through those first teary fittings. You were so comforting and reassuring that I snapped right back into enjoying the whole thing! You've given me an amazing gift that I'll remember forever and the gown was just heaven to wear!

Love,
Aimee Reynolds

Your Tux Rental Specialist

Dear Ryan,

Thank you so much for your advice and help in dressing our handsome men! We loved the tuxes you helped us find and the men were complimented all day! And yes, we caught most of them checking themselves out in the mirror! You have a fabulous eye, and we're so glad we worked with you.

With all best wishes,
Tom and Claire Angelino

Your Travel Agent

Dear Vanessa,

Thank you, thank you, thank you for your wonderful help in planning our honeymoon—and we so appreciate all the work you did setting up our group discount for our guests' travel, too! Thanks to you, so many of our loved ones could be there for the wedding! That meant the world to us! It was a pleasure working with you, and we'll look forward to coming back to you for our future vacation plans!

All the best,
Maya and Jim Downs

Your Officiant

Dear Reverend Thomas,

Thank you for your guidance in planning our ceremony and for being open to our ideas! We loved working with you; we appreciated your counsel, and you did a marvelous job at our ceremony. Your readings meant so much to us, and the words of the day will stay with us always.

Our thanks and best wishes,
Tom and Sarah Richards

Dear Father Chilton,

We wanted to write with our gratitude for the joyous and beautiful ceremony you conducted for our wedding last weekend. We loved the words you spoke, the smile in your eyes as you read our vows and the joy with which you announced us as husband and wife. Please convey our thanks to your staff and musicians, the organist and choir! Everyone made our ceremony the faith-filled and lovely start that we prayed for.

All the best,
Caroline and Marvin Kelly

CHAPTER 18

To Your Own Children

If you have children of your own, the past few months may have been a blur of activity for them. Maybe they've really amazed you with their willingness to help, their talent, their support and their excitement about the wedding to come.

No matter the child's age or involvement level, it's a wonderful idea for the two of you to thank your offspring with a heartfelt note and perhaps a gift as well. While many parents run to the jewelry store to buy a diamond pendant or heart locket, or to the stadium for season tickets to a pro sport team, it's not the gift that matters right now. It's the words you share with each son or daughter who's a blessing to you.

The Right Words for the Kids

When writing your kids, you're not just thanking them for giving up the senior class trip to attend your wedding, or wielding the glue gun to help make your invitations. It goes much further than that, as now is the perfect time to share the sentiments that so many parents *wish* they'd taken the time to give to their kids. You'll thank them for the wonderful people they have turned out to be, how they amaze you every day with their talents or faith or wisdom, how you have unconditional love for them, how they make it so easy to love them, how proud a departed parent would be right now. Words on paper, written in your own hand, give you that golden moment in time to speak what's in your heart—something that, quite regrettably, many people are just not able to do.

Your children will treasure your thank-you note more than you can imagine. It's a love note that often becomes a most prized possession, something your kids show their own kids someday. In many ways, this could be one of the most important thank-you notes you'll write, as it becomes part of the legacy of love in your own family circle.

Dear Joshua,

Even though things are very busy right now, there's not a moment that goes by that I don't think about how YOU are my greatest gift on earth. I'm so happy for this new chapter in our lives, and it makes me elated that you are as well. I've always been proud of you, even when you were a little boy, and no gift could ever make me more fulfilled than being your mother. As Gary and I take this next step, it's all the sweeter knowing how much you love Gary as well. And that he loves you more than he can express sometimes. Every mom dreams of the fairy tale come true, and mine is better than I could have ever hoped. My son is a wonderful man who makes the world a better place, and it's my wish that all of your dreams come true.

Always with love, with my whole heart,
Mom

Dear Kristin,

Every mom should be so lucky as to have a daughter like you! I may not have had much time lately, but the best moments in planning this wedding have been our girls' nights, surfing the Web to laugh at the ugly bridesmaid dresses, making our hot cocoa, and I still laugh when I think of your very creative "worst songs to dance a first dance to" list! You make my day, every day, full of sunshine and light, and you are an absolute treasure to me. I love you with all of my heart, and this new future in front of me and Stephen is all the brighter because you're going to be at the center of it. You're the best gift we have.

All my love, forever,
Mom

For Kids Who Are Too Young to Read

Just because your child is a baby or isn't old enough to appreciate a great, tear-jerking letter, you should still write the note, date it, and store it safely for a future sharing when your son or daughter is old enough. It will mean so much to know that you took pen to paper now, that you had such loving and grateful thoughts, even when the child in question was an infant...or perhaps not yet born. Sometimes just the smile of a baby, or a flutter in your stomach, a dream of the future, is more than enough to warrant the deepest *thank you* possible.

Dear Jackson,

I've been on the receiving end of a lot of celebration lately, and while those gifts and parties are nice, they don't measure up to the celebration and gifts I've experienced from being your father. I may not say it often enough, but I look at you with pure pride in the solid man you have become. You've shown a lot of growth this year, from accepting my upcoming marriage to welcoming Tania into our family, to guiding your brothers and sisters into this transition as well. Without you, I wouldn't have this happiness in my heart. You're my right hand, and I love you more than a million times saying it could even begin to do it justice. The future I'm equally excited about is yours, to see where the road takes you, to see how much more you'll amaze me with your smarts, your strength and that sense of humor. Thank you for being such a great son, my boy. And thank you for allowing me to be the best father I can be to you. I look at my other friends and I know I'm blessed to have a son who is so easy to love, and who's strong enough to show love in return. No father has ever been more thankful . . .

Love always,
Dad

PART FOUR

Ordering (or Making) Thank-You Notes

You have a choice: Will you order or make your thank-you notes? Some couples order their thank-you-note card sets together with their wedding invitation packets; some order them custom-made from a professional graphic artist or stationery company, others design and print their own on the home computer. Here, you'll find out all you need to know to make your choices wisely, shop smartly and design with complete details to make the finished product look lovely—no matter where or how you created them.

From pretty papers to colored vellums to stamp-accented monograms and envelope sizes and shapes, you'll have all the information you need to create thank-you notes that stand out and express your personalities as well as your gratitude.

CHAPTER 19

Professionally Made Thank Yous

While many couples choose the professionally made thank-you notes that match their wedding invitations—and are part of the package in the same paper type and matching font and color—others choose from several different sources:

- Thank-you notes ordered from a catalog supplied by their wedding photographer—to get their pick of a pretty photo-window card to show off their bridal portrait

- Picture-window thank-you notes ordered online from a bridal website

- Picture-window notes from a photography supplies and specialty photo albums site like www.exposuresonline.com

- Regular thank-you notes, in a separate style from the invitation's style, from an invitations catalog in a stationery store

- Regular thank-you notes, in a separate style from the invitation's style, from online invitations sites. (See the Resources at the back of this book for companies to check out.)

- Custom thank-you notes from artisans who design and make your notes in-house

As you can see, you'll find a range of packages, from basic matching sets (sometimes for free when you match to your invitation style) to pricier custom creations. It's up to you to decide where you'll shop and how much you'll spend for your choice of design. You don't have to match your invitation style if you don't wish to, and you can order several different styles of thank-you notes for different occasions, such as for your shower (where you might choose a more city-chic design) or for your parents and bridal party members after the wedding. You might want to send them something a little more special and personalized than the standard printed thank-you notes you'll send to the rest of your guests. It's completely up to you.

You can, of course, purchase preprinted thank-you notes from the card store, or order preprinted thank-you notes online. The range of design styles out there is immense and inspiring, with some fabulous artistry to choose from. Romantic, Tuscany-inspired, art deco, colorful, black-and-white . . . you'll find them all.

Or, you may decide to custom-order your thank-you notes, which you'll build from scratch, limited only by your imagination.

In this section, you'll think about the details of your professionally created thank-you notes. Just as you did with your wedding invitations, you have some artistic choices ahead of you: font style, color of ink, paper style and color. It's all the fun once again, giving you another chance to personalize your design.

Finding the Perfect Professional

Of course, your product is only going to come out great if done by a reputable company with a long track record in phenomenal art and professionalism. So ask your friends to recommend the invitation or printing companies they used; it's often the best way to find the ideal source. I've listed my favorites within this chapter and highly recommend them for their customer service, beautiful work, quick delivery and terrific prices. The criteria you should look for when choosing a company to order from are:

- A great range of designs and wording templates

- Ease of creation—meaning that the process is painless, your ideas are heard and implemented and if online, that the creation process is easy to navigate

- A printer who will send you a print proof on the actual paper used for the final product. This is very important, as an e-mailed version won't give you the feel of the paper (of course) and a regular print copy on laser paper also won't give you that authentic appearance. (The proof may be free, or it may cost a nominal amount, which I recommend investing in.)

- A great range of fonts, and the ability to use two different fonts for free (instead of being charged for the secondary print appearance)

- A stylist who will show you the full listing of fonts, letting you know if any font comes out as hard to read. Some Ms look like Ns, for instance, and Os look like 9s. A true professional will show you the font listing in its entirety and will advise you about letter quality.

- Fair prices (Extra fees should be clear, and the fine print should be acceptable to you.)

- Shipping by a well-known shipping company, with tracking and the option of insurance

- Online ordering that's safety-protected

- The ability to add graphics, perhaps for free, and guidance about resolution and the sending of digital images

- In the case of online companies, a street address for their office, identifying them as more of a legitimate business

- A satisfactory projected shipment date, knowing it will take a matter of days or weeks, not months

Get Your Terminology Straight

There are a variety of choices available to you as you decide upon your stationery. If you learn to speak your invitation expert's language, you'll save time in the ordering process, and get exactly what you want.

Paper Type

100 percent cotton: Among the most elegant and formal types of paper, a top traditional choice

Corrugated: A thicker paper with ridges and wrinkles; touchable texture

Deckled edge: A thicker paper with edges that look torn and ridged

Handmade paper: An artistic version of paper that is handmade, with texture and often embedded flowers or confetti. The most common forms are organic cotton materials, plant fibers, even hemp.

Industrial paper: Very similar to corrugated, this style is thicker, edged, grooved and wrinkled. May also come in textured parchment.

Jacquard: A paper "illusion" with the texture of lace or other design built into the paper, giving it a unique feel

Laid: A thinner but textured paper, with a raised and slightly bumpy finish

Linen: One of the most popular choices for thank-you notes and invitations. Provides a slightly more textured appearance than 100 percent cotton and is the paper of choice for formal printed papers.

Marble: Artistic design paper with a marble graphic, semi-stripes of color in swirled or horizontal lines or arcs to resemble Italian marble in a range of colors

Matte: As with any matte finish, this paper comes without a shine to it.

Parchment: Either a thicker, old-fashioned off-white paper, or a thinner translucent version for a unique note foundation

Rice paper: Thinner and softer than traditional papers, it's a popular choice for its crisp appearance. Contrary to popular belief, there's no rice in the paper itself, and its formation lends well to a coloring process. Note, though, that rice paper does not work well with all printing processes. It's best with letterpress, as it's not thick enough to hold engraving or thermography.

Vellum: A thin, translucent paper made with a cotton blend that gives it an airier, see-through look in a range of shades and textures. Usually used as a decorative overlay page to printed wedding items but can hold print if you'd like to add words or graphics to it.

Paper Color

This one is completely up to you. You can go with bridal white or ecru; soft blushes in pinks, blues, lilacs, yellows or creamsicle oranges; brights in reds and oranges; deep jewel tones such as sapphires and emeralds; metallics such as copper or gold. Using color in your thank-you-note paper is the new hot trend, giving it a shot of visual excitement, even if it's the thank-you from a formal wedding for which you sent traditional ivory invitations. Colored borders or pearlized edging is perfectly fine, as you'll find plenty of opportunities to edge your cards with color or texture.

As an added color kick, you don't have to match the paper color to the envelope color. Some of the prettiest thank-you notes I've seen created for couples featured orange cards in hot-pink envelopes; hunter-green cards in sage-green envelopes; purple cards in lavender envelopes and deep blue cards in sky-blue envelopes.

Font Style

As you know, your font is the style of print, the artistic design in the lettering itself. When you work with a professional to create your thank-you notes, you'll choose the style of font you desire just like you would when ordering business cards or letterhead for work. Look through the full examples lineup for each font you like, and be sure that each letter is clear, each number legible. Some fonts are so artistic, they can be hard to decipher. For your thank-you notes, it won't be the numbers as much as the letters that matter most (as you might remember from doing your invitations and making sure that 1 P.M.

doesn't look like 7 P.M. . . . or your guests would be six hours late for your wedding!).

You'll find *thousands* of highly stylized possibilities from company to company. So look online at their lists of available fonts, and know that invitations experts can e-mail or fax you their own font lists in full detail.

Font Color

When it comes to font color, you have your choice of shade mixes, but make sure that the print is legible. You might just need to bold up your color for this, so that a red print really shows up on a pink background, for instance. Silver print on darker-colored paper is a new trend, especially for winter weddings, and traditional black print on colored paper is always a rock-solid choice. Talk with your professional note designer about pricing differences for using colored fonts, as well as which colors are available for the fonts you have in mind. Not all fonts come in all colors; you may have to select from an existing list of possibilities for each.

Printing Method

The printing method works just as it did for your wedding invitations. Certain print methods are more formal (such as engraving, where your letters are actually die-stamped into the paper to reveal raised letters with indentations on the back of the paper; this is the most formal and expensive form of printing). When you're ordering professionally made thank-you notes, the print method is one of the most important and fundamental decisions you'll make to guide your choices, so consider the following options:

Blind-embossing: Your letters will be raised, but will have no color hue to them. Letter forms are stamped into your paper, giving you a raised letter texture. This print method is often used for monograms at the top of your note.

Calligraphy: Ornate handwritten script in a range of styles

Embossing: Same as blind-embossing above, with the raised letters and textures, only color may be a part of it

Engraving: Again, the most formal and expensive of printing methods. A steel die is used to impress each letter of your note into a raised surface with an indentation on the back.

Letterpress: Also an expensive method, this one presses the paper against the inked image so that your print appears embedded in the paper, not raised or indented. Artists prefer this method for textured papers.

Offset: Produces flat lettering and is growing into one of the most popular choices today for its crisp quality and inexpensive pricing.

Thermography: The most popular choice right now for all professionally-printed items, this method uses heat and a fusing resin to create raised letters with no indentations on the back of the card. This lettering also has a shine to it, giving an extra-special quality to a print that *looks* like it's engraved but isn't.

Vellums and Embellishments

Your thank-you note can be covered with a slip of iridescent or translucent vellum if you wish, hole punched at the top or corners to give an artistic touch to it, stamped with your monogram at the top or bottom or hole-punched at the top with a color-coordinated ribbon bow. It's the little extras that make a note stand out, and the cost for such embellishments is very low.

It's out of style now to include confetti of any kind in a thank-you note, as that touch has grown into a cultural annoyance, serving no purpose other than causing your recipient to have to vacuum it up from the floor. Skip it. It's a waste of time and money, and it's considered tacky right now.

CHAPTER 20

Making Your Own Thank Yous

If you choose to make your own stylish thank-you notes using your home computer and printer, the advice in the previous chapter applies here as well. Making your own cards is a hot trend right now, and couples love playing "print designer" as they personalize their own notes with colors, graphics, borders, fun fonts, and their own wording. The result is a thank-you note design that's one of a kind, a job that's done in a day rather than a month, and a substantial savings to the budget.

You could spend a few hundred dollars on professionally made thank-you notes, or you could spend less than fifty dollars on supplies for a do-it-yourself job. That, combined with total creative control, is the allure behind making your own notes. In this chapter, you'll find some of my favorite resources and supplies for this task, as current trends in customizing homemade thank-you notes.

Software

One software option is using the word-processing program on your home computer. Most couples who go the do-it-yourself route enjoy the freedom of using the color options, a range of fonts, clip art graphics, their own digital photos or other details as covered in this chapter. Another option is to buy an inexpensive software program that offers you easy-to-use templates, fun and updated fonts and graphics and a step-by-step guide that takes the guesswork out of alignment, centering and other layout issues. (After all, graphic designers and artists go to school to learn this stuff, so a great software package allows you the same design capabilities without years of study.)

While the Resource section contains a sampling of different packages to consider, my choice of software program is Printing Press Platinum by Mountaincow.com, which has modern graphics and unique, original fonts. Their Flourish Monogram and Classic Monogram especially stand out among all other designs for their decidedly contemporary and sophisticated feel.

This program and other stationery-printing software feature fun graphics like martini glasses, flowers, stilettos (perfect for shower thank yous), snowflakes and more for the perfect design elements on your cards. Your homemade notes will far outshine those made by couples who used their computer's basic, outdated clip art.

When you're considering any stationery-printing software program, be sure it features a tool to import your Outlook address book, a spell-checker, and a tool to keep track of your thank-you-note progress.

Card Stock

Look back at the advice in chapter 19 on card stock (linens, laids, jacquards, etc.) and then head to the office supply store to find your perfect papers. Look at the different colors and card thicknesses to select

---

A Sampling of International Papers

When you start looking online for unique, imported papers, you're going to discover a whole new world with exotic and delicious terms to speak aloud, let alone order. Consider the following papers: Velata, Annigone, Pescia, Papyrus, Himalayan Lokta, Thai Handmade Kozo, Mitsumata, Hosho, Kinwashi, Tamarind. It's like another language, indeed! The custom of paper-making goes way back in exotic lands, and you'll be on the receiving end of finely crafted papers that make the words on your thank-you notes seem like a delicacy. While the custom of papers embedded with floral bits is going out of style, you'll still find amazing designs of papers with *whole* dried flowers embedded: cornflower, marigold, rose petals, yellow star petals. Paper design is a fascinating and beautiful world, so see if you can bring in an international touch to your notes. See the Resources section for more on artistic paper sources.

---

the perfect card type *that will work in your home computer printer.* Some printers are fussy and will give you a hard time with unique papers like wispy vellums and thicker cardboard types.

Once you know your printer can handle it (details should be in your owner's manual), you should have a wide range of papers and card stocks to choose from. Most couples look at the heavier paper weights of greeting card stock or presentation papers, going a little bit thicker than the usual laser printer paper. In the stationery aisle, you'll find marbled paper, parchments in a range of colors, brights and pastels, pre-bordered card stock, fun and kicky design-printed cards, soft gloss and regular gloss papers for a bit of shine and recycled papers. Be open while walking through that aisle, and buy enough of your chosen card stock style to make 25 percent more thank-you notes than you'll need (leaving room for mistakes discovered while printing).

Of course, you can upgrade your paper stock by going to an art supply store or ordering from a fine paper source online, choosing imported papers from Thailand, Morocco, Japan, South Africa, Argentina and other locales. Rice papers are always in high demand for their unusual feel, for instance. Professional invitation designers go to these same stores and online sources for their own eye-catching paper supplies, so your homemade notes will have the same impressive feel as those made by the pros.

Vellums and Overlays

You may choose to cover your thank-you note with a lovely translucent vellum, tissue paper or other overlay. In the past, these overlays were placed over printed wedding invitations to protect the ink on the card. As print methods improved and heat became a part of the printing process, the vellums weren't quite needed but still stayed as a matter of tradition and style. You can include these as more of a design touch to your thank-you notes, for an added layer of color and visual impact. You'll find vellums in your office supply store, arts and crafts stores and online in a wide range of new and modern designs such as winter snowflake themes; soft, barely-there floral themes; marbles; ocean wave ripples; pure solid color and more.

Font Style

Again, a great software package will open up a whole new world of print design to you, taking you away from the usually-seen fonts on a home computer. But even if you don't wish to invest in software, you'll certainly be able to explore that lengthy list of fonts on your word-processing program, alter them further with italics and bolds, see how they look in a different color or size and customize your notes to the degree that your recipients *think* you used a professional.

You can use more than one type of font—one for your card front and another for the printed inside wording—but keep it to two types of fonts only or your card will look more like a ransom note with letters of all shapes and sizes. And remember to always hand-sign your names on your personalized note.

Print Color

Color choice is completely yours to make! You can use any range of font color offered on your home computer or software, or go classic and elegant with black. If you don't have a color printer, use a friend's or get permission to use the office printer.

I've been focusing on computer-generated thank-you notes a lot, but this is one place where I want to discuss handwritten notes, too. You'll find a wide range of interesting pens, from gel colored inks to calligraphy pens to splashy silver-ink markers, in office supply or craft stores. Consider giving your handwritten messages an extra flash of color by using a great, unique pen rather than a black ballpoint. You don't need to learn how to do calligraphy to use a calligraphy pen . . . the new styles of pre-slanted pens come in a range of colors and give a design style to your own everyday handwriting.

Again, stick with two colors maximum, as the rainbow print look will likely come off as too juvenile. Use one darker and one lighter coordinating color palette if you do wish to mix color in your writing.

Borders

From a single, elegant black line around the outskirts of your card to a thicker border in a green ivy design, graphic borders can add an extra design touch to cards you make. Whether you get them from your home computer or from your digital camera software program, you can play artist with various borders to see how your wording looks within the surrounding design. Never use a border that outshines your words.

Graphics

Graphics can be used in and on your cards. For instance, instead of enclosing your wedding portrait within the card or displaying it in a traditional picture-window card, you can upload your wedding portrait to be printed *on* the card. Better yet, you can choose a more customized photo, such as one from your first dance. You have your choice of bridal photos to use, even the one with cake smashed on your faces.

Beyond the bridal photo, you can also click and paste into your card design any number of graphics you love, such as a gerbera daisy or a sunset, a starfish or a single red rose. The choices are up to you, made easier by your computer's software such as the ability to capture an image from a stock photo website and insert it right into your design. Depending on the style of your thank-you note, you might decide to go more formal, without graphics, or fun and playful with stylized images. It's completely up to you, which is the beauty of the create-your-own thank-you-note design. What are the top choices in customized graphics used on thank-you notes? I asked 1,000 brides and grooms through my website, and the results are as follows:

1. A sunset over the ocean

2. A pair of filled wineglasses and candles

3. Florals

4. Doves

5. Ferns and leaves

No entwined rings in sight. Ditto for wedding bells. Today's couples are choosing images that are a far cry from the pictures on their parents' wedding invitations, with more images from nature or from their lifestyles. So give yourself the freedom to step away from "bridal" pictures to those that point to who you are as a couple.

Embellishments

I also asked the same 1,000 wedding couples how they planned to embellish or decorate their homemade thank-you notes. The majority said they'd use their monogram at the top or bottom. Your monogram is the entwined letters of your first names and last name, such as AMC. New twists on the monogram include using lowercase letters, and also using fun and modern fonts for the monogram.

Other top choices, easily made with supplies you'll find at the craft store or office supply store:

1. Hole punches in the shapes of hearts or shooting stars, even circles of different sizes

2. A hole punch at the top with a color-coordinated ribbon tied in a bow
   [Note: This one is just like the embellishment so many couples are purchasing with their professionally made thank-you notes and invitations—it's no wonder the Do-It-Yourself crowd is embracing the trend!]

3. Foil stickers

4. Wax seals (to seal the envelopes; use a wax seal kit from the craft store, where you can purchase a seal stamp in your monogram letter)

5. Hand-drawn artwork (if you're the artistic type)

You might consider using scrapbooking supplies from the craft store. If you're not familiar with the tools of this fast-growing hobby, get

---

What Does Revlon Have to Do with It?

A top trend in thank-you-note adornment? Particularly for shower thank yous, it's the lipstick kiss print. Made by you.

---

thee to the craft store right now! You'll find the most amazing cutouts on colored paper that can be glued to your notes. I *love* the strips of textured mini starfish and mini daisies that can be cut to measure and then affixed to the top or bottom lengths of your card. Other options: mini dots affixed in random patterns on a colored card stock note; textured stickers as the top feature of a note; pearlized border stickers and so on. It's so incredibly easy and inexpensive to give a textured, customized look to your card with the stylized paper and sticker products available in the scrapbooking world.

Your Printing Process

You're probably no stranger to a computer and printer, so I won't bore you with the basics. Just be sure to test-print your first copy and inspect it closely for any mistakes. See if the ink smears on your card stock from the pass-through of the card coming up behind it. And store your cards safely away from kids and pets once they're printed and ready for your signing and sealing session.

CHAPTER 21

Stamp Art

When you completed your wedding invitation packets, you added the special "finishing touch" with a pretty postage stamp, perhaps a LOVE stamp or two. It made for a lovely presentation, something special in your guests' pile of just-arrived mail. Now, for your thank-you notes, you can do the same.

You might choose to use the exact same type of LOVE postage stamp that you used on your invitations, bringing the matching set of wedding stationery full-circle, or you might choose to go unique and themed with your postage stamps. Your choice might reflect the location of your wedding such as a garden bouquet of pink and white flowers to remind guests of your beautiful garden wedding, or the Pacific coral reef to bring them back to your destination wedding in Hawaii.

Or maybe your stamp will reflect your interests, such as the series of American choreographer stamps, which would also remind guests of the great night of dancing they enjoyed at your reception, or the series of 1950s classic car stamps because you rode up in a gleaming Corvette convertible on your wedding day. Or, your stamp might reflect your cherished causes, such as the extra-postage breast cancer stamp for which a donation is made to the fight against cancer. In this instance, your stamp gives a little bit back to the world.

The list of themed postage stamps is extensive, and you'll find lists and pictures of them at the United States Post Office website (www.usps.gov). Just click on to search their categories, and—very important—to make sure that the stamp you have in mind *is* qualified as a postage stamp and not just a collector's item. Not all stamps are viable for the job as postage, so look for a capitalized or bolded disclaimer in the listing of each.

I encourage you to explore the Postal Service's website, especially looking at their list of upcoming releases (click on "Release Schedules"). You might just discover that with a few weeks' wait, you'll be able to use the perfect themed stamp, the newly released LOVE stamp, or a commemorative stamp of a great artist, dancer, author or inspirational personality.

While any plain postage stamp will do the job of getting your thank-you notes from here to there, you can personalize your mailing with the perfect touch in a more creative choice.

Return Address Labels

It's so easy and inexpensive to order return address labels, so why not order your new collection now? You'll first decide how you and your spouse would like your names to read in formality. Will you be *Mr. and Mrs. Jeffrey Smith? Mr. and Mrs. Jeff Smith? Anne and Jeff Smith?* These are labels you'll use far longer than for this particular task of sending thank-you notes, so make your decision based on what works best for your upcoming daily life.

As far as etiquette goes, you'll use a label with *both* of your names on it, since the thank-you note is from the two of you. It's not considered proper for you to use just one of your names on the return label alone (even if you're among the minority who writes out all the thank yous without the help of your spouse). Your wedding guests came to see both of you, gifts were given to the both of you, so the thank you is from the both of you. It sounds like a petty, trivial issue, but this is one area the firm grasp of etiquette rules is not going to let go of anytime soon.

Old Address or New?

Return address labels can pose a challenge to couples who expect to move into a new home after the wedding but don't yet have the actual place. Your solution? Obviously, you'll order return labels for the address you're at now and will send an official change of address card or e-mail notification later. Of course, if you do have papers signed on your new apartment, condo or house, then you'll use the new return address label as well as sending out an official At-Home card (which allows you to share your new phone number and e-mail as well. See chapter 24 on At-Home cards for more details, and see the Resources section on great sources for professional label-design companies). Ordering new address labels then gives you an extra thrill as well—you have *a new home*, too!

Matching Colors?

Depending on how color-coordinated you wish to be with your thank-you-note envelopes, you could order labels to match the color of your postage stamps. Again, you'll find mightily discounted offers for labels online and in those coupon packets that arrive in the mail seemingly every week. So it might be your style and taste to choose a sage-green address label to go nicely with the sage green of the postage stamp you love. Consider colors and how the envelope presentation will look, and of course there are always clear labels that allow you future freedom in this regard.

Bride and Groom Specialty Labels

In the world of specialty labels (easily found online at bridal websites) you can find cute return address labels complete with illustrations of cherub-faced brides and grooms, or a white rose in a graphics block on the left edge of the label. You'll also find JUST MARRIED! written above your names in elegant script, images of wedding bells, doves, wedding rings, champagne bottles, any bridal image you can imagine.

Some companies will personalize the corner images on your labels, using graphics of the two of you from your wedding day, with the label slightly enlarged to suit the size of the graphic. It might be a square, for instance, instead of a traditional rectangle, even a larger oval or circle. You can also find sources that will personalize an illustration of the two of you, or allow you to choose from hundreds of face, hair and eye colors and styles so that the image looks quite like you both.

Decide if you wish to invest in a roll of these specialty labels. It could be the fun, bridal touch you always wanted, and the graphics really grab the eye. Check out the Resources section for companies that design these and other specialty labels.

The Sticker on the Back

The back side of the envelope shouldn't be neglected! While you should avoid sticker overkill, a classic and elegant monogram sticker makes a lovely seal on the back. Check at craft and office supply stores for your choice of single-initial monogram stickers, or you may also order your own pack of personalized monogram stickers for all of your future correspondence.

How do you arrange the letters in your personalized monogram? Jeff and Anne Smith's would be as follows, with their last initial enlarged and centered, and their first initials on either side. It's their choice which side they'd like their initial on:

$$J \, S \, A$$

Obviously, if your names in monogram form aren't quite presentable (such as Andrew and Sarah Smith), and if you care about that sort of thing, you might choose to switch the order or just stick with the single monogram.

CHAPTER 22

Envelope Smarts

We've just covered affixing stamps to your envelopes, and now it's time to talk about how you'll fill them out. Do you have to be as formal with these envelopes as with your wedding invitation envelopes, where you spelled out the word *Street* and *District of Columbia?* Can it get a little more informal than that now? Absolutely. You can abbreviate the usuals *if you wish to.* You can, as a matter of your personal preference if you had a formal or ultra-formal wedding, still use the ultra-formal wording rules for your envelopes. No one is going to get angry or offended either way. (Finally! A little relief from the strict rules!)

You will, of course, address the thank you to the givers:

- If the gift was from Mr. and Mrs. Sean O'Donnelly, you'll put *Mr. and Mrs. Sean O'Donnelly* on the envelope, and then write in "Dear Mary and Sean" inside their card.

- If the gift was from Mr. and Mrs. Sean O'Donnelly and their kids Justin, Joshua, Kelly and Amanda, you may write *Mr. and Mrs. Sean O'Donnelly and Family* or

  Mr. and Mrs. Sean O'Donnelly
  Justin, Joshua, Kelly and Amanda

  on the envelope front. That's your choice, and you may address them all by name inside the card as well. Kids love seeing their names on "important mail." It makes them feel included and honored.

- If a wedding guest came with a date, you'll address the thank-you note to both of them, sent to the one address of the guest you originally invited. There's no need to send the date a separate thank-you note.

- Full addresses are used, and you can check on a zip code you're unsure of at www.usps.gov.

- If a guest lives temporarily at home with parents, or with a relative or friend while his house is being remodeled, you'll send it to him as follows:

  Mr. Brian Paulison
  c/o Mr. and Mrs. Thomas Everson
  111 Main Street
  Dover Falls, NY 00000

- Use complete coding and accurate numbers when sending thank-you notes to foreign countries and islands so that they are received in good time.

- Never use stickers or clear labels to affix addresses to envelopes. Yes, these can be less formal, and mail-merge programs using your address book take the time out of the job, but it just looks tacky. Either address your envelopes by hand, or feed your envelopes through your printer for a more elegant and polished look. (Just be sure to test one envelope first, as some printers' heat mechanism can seal your envelopes during the printing process.)

Square Envelopes, Oversized Envelopes and Extra-Postage Issues

When using square or oversized envelopes, you may run into problems with extra postage. Whenever you're using a larger size or a square shape that falls outside the boundaries of the Postal Service's rules for postage, take a trip to the post office for the clerk's official test on the scale, at which point you'll know the rules for your collection of thank-you notes.

That is, of course, the easiest way to explore the issue, but if you have questions about the rules for envelope dimensions, visit the Postal Service's website, www.usps.gov, for a size and weight calculator that's easy to use, particularly if you'll be sending out thank-you *packages* containing a CD-ROM or other gift rather than a flat envelope.

Of course, if your envelope contains a thank-you note with a raised element (such as a ribbon tied into a bow at the top), you'll need to have your notes hand-stamped at the post office. These types of raises and bumps in an envelope can cause it to jam in the system's processing machinery. Again, check with your mail clerk for verification.

Mailing Boxes

As mentioned earlier, you may have taken a more creative route with your thank yous, mailing out CD-ROMs in jewel cases with a video message from the two of you, a compilation of your wedding-day images, or a gift you'll send along with your thank-you notes. In these cases, presentation with your mailing box is quite important. You might not want to go with a standard mailing box from the post office, one with PRIORITY MAIL written on it in red, white and blue, and you may not want to use a standard bubble mailer in canary yellow from the office supply store.

You can find terrific white and colored mailing boxes and flats at office supply stores and websites (*see* the Resources section). As you practiced with your wedding, the little touches are key, and checking out your options can inspire terrific ideas on sending something special through the mail.

Other sources for great box wrapping: the gift-box display case at your favorite music store. Here, you'll find wrapping-friendly boxes and self-seal flat wrappers for DVDs and VHS that come in a variety of designs: elegant and classic, such as a tuxedo box with a red rose, or bright and artsy like a hologram of red and pink stripes. Your local craft and paper supply stores will also stock terrific wrapping boxes and envelopes that you can use as-is or enhance yourself with graphics you'll print out on your home computer. Whatever your design, be sure your mailing label is large, plain and easy to read by the Postal Service. No silver pen scribbled on red hologram mailers.

PART FIVE

Inserts

The official wedding portrait has long been a traditional insert in wedding thank-you notes, and the practice continues . . . but with a twist. Now you have the freedom to include a *fun* photo such as the two of you dancing or smiling with cake frosting on your noses. Your picture can be as expressive as you wish, traditional or creative. Here, you'll make your plans for the portrait you'd love to use, and even how you can save money by doing it yourself.

You're not limited to just a picture, however. As you'll see in this section, you can also insert a favorite quote printed on parchment, or a poem on a laminated card that inspires you or makes you laugh. To make life easier on yourselves and your guests, you can also enclose an At-Home card with your new address, phone number and e-mail so that all of your loved ones can find you after the wedding. Read on to start your plans for what you can insert in your thank-you notes.

CHAPTER 23

Your Wedding Portrait

Traditionally, many brides and grooms have ordered from their photographers a hundred or so wallet-sized color prints of their official wedding portrait, the best photo of them smiling on their wedding day in full bridal regalia. They've either slipped the photo into their thank-you notes, or they've chosen a card with a picture window cut-out to show off the snapshot. Guests love receiving this picture, and it often goes right up on the refrigerator. So important is this official shot of your day that guests are either disappointed or offended if they don't receive one. What's being done today is a little bit different. While many couples are still using the formal, side-by-side, posed couple shot with both of them beaming and their hands subtly showing off the rings, others are choosing a *different* photo. One that's less posed and more *them*. After all, weddings are far more personalized now. Some couples request that all of their photos be candids, action shots, with no stiff posed photos in sight. This opens up a wonderful world to you. Your thank-you-note portrait could possibly be:

- The two of you during your first dance, singing to one another, smiling, looking into one another's eyes

- Your groom kissing your hand as you look adoringly at him

- A kissing shot by your wedding cake

- A kissing shot with your bridal bouquet held just below your chins

- The moment he dramatically dips you during your spotlight dance

- The two of you clinking champagne flutes

- A celebratory pose, with the two of you standing on the edge of a beautiful fountain, holding hands above your heads, smiling and laughing

- The perfect garden scene, with you sitting on a cobblestone wall and him offering you a single rose

- The two of you splashing in the ocean's edge, your dress held up from the water and his pant cuffs rolled up

- The two of you sitting in the sand on the beach, showing your love of the beach and your playfulness

- The two of you captured during the dash to the limo, with rose petals falling all around you

- The two of you standing up through the limousine's sunroof, or a shot of the two of you waving out the back window of that Bentley or Rolls-Royce, the JUST MARRIED sign bordered by beautiful flowers

Your options are endless, open to full creation as you consider what image suits you best, what's most *you*. It could be the perfect reflection

Does the Picture Have to Be from the Wedding?

Usually, it is a wedding-day photo, but more couples are sending great pictures from their honeymoons. Especially if they had a honeymoon registry and many of their guests contributed to their getaway of a lifetime, that shot of the two of them in the azure-blue tropical waters, swimming with dolphins or kissing next to a waterfall shares an unforgettable image with loved ones.

of your relationship to have a smiling, laughing shot with cake frosting dotted on your noses during your cake-cutting ritual, or a more romantic shot of the two of you walking hand in hand down the beach as the sun sets gloriously ahead of you. The photographer is looking for your wished-for shot, so get creative, think outside the box and choose a photo that shares the ideal image with your guests.

Using Different Photos for Different Groups

It may take a little bit more organization, but you can customize your photo to the recipient by groups. For instance, the thank-you notes you'll send to your bridal party members will include not just that great shot of the two of you, but also a great shot of your bridal party members with you, posed or a candid shot. For your parents' thank-you notes, you can include that beautiful picture of you with all of your parents and stepparents. For the thank-you note to your flower girl, send that priceless photo of the two of you dancing together, or posing together in the garden. You can tuck in an extra shot to any special recipients, such as grandparents or favorite great-aunts, friends and the couple who introduced the two of you. It's your choice to make, and your thank-you note is the perfect place for such a thoughtful enclosure. This is where thank-you-note enclosures benefit from the personalized nature of weddings today . . . you can personalize them right down to the photo you send.

Printing Photos Yourselves

If you choose to print your photos yourself, you might pick a great digital photo from your own camera at the ceremony or reception, upload it at an inexpensive photo developing site (like www.kodakgallery.com, or Target's or Costco's photo developing centers) and print out your own desired number of pictures. I suggest these types of inexpensive alternatives, particularly because you can easily edit, crop, border and color-fix your own photos on your home computer to get just the perfect image.

What I *don't* suggest is sending cheap-looking color photocopies of your picture on regular printer paper, complete with a wavy, scissor-cut job on the edges. While it's a great intention to share pictures from your day, sending a guest—particularly one who traveled far to attend and gave you a generous gift—a poor-quality photocopy lacks in finesse. Check at your office supply store for glossy photo paper and if you print out your own images, use impressive paper stock such as this. And cut cleanly with a straight-line paper cutter. It may seem trivial, but it really does make a difference. Your home-done job can look extremely professional for pennies.

CHAPTER 24

At-Home Cards

A big trend in thank-you notes right now is enclosing an At-Home card, *even if you haven't moved anywhere after the wedding.* Sharing your home address, phone and e-mail on this official card enclosure is more than a service to your friends and family, allowing them to keep in touch with you—it's an invitation to them as well, asking them to keep in touch with you. It's a gesture of closeness.

While most of your close friends and family know your address and e-mail, not all of them do. Many brides and grooms tell me that the simple act of enclosing an At-Home card led to their becoming closer to some family members, for example, planning Cousins' Night Out and other get-togethers soon after the honeymoon. Many couples have told me that they're more "in the loop" with family news when great-aunts who have e-mail (who knew!?) send the best letters with family updates and photos. Old friends you found through a search engine in order to invite to your wedding are also invited into your world as a re-connection that's been long overdue. Since today's weddings are all about connecting with loved ones, life after the wedding is richer when you're in closer touch with relatives and friends.

The At-Home card is where everyone will learn about your name change, or lack thereof. When they see *Kelly Jones-Smith* on the card, they'll know that you hyphenated. Or that you prefer to be called *Kelly Jones*. Or—as we're seeing in growing numbers—that your groom has modified his last name with a hyphenation of his own. Whichever option you choose for yourselves, you'll announce it on your At-Home card so that guests can address you properly in the future.

Getting your wording right is far less involved than with your invitations or thank yous. It could be a matter of just following the traditional format below, or personalizing your At-Home card with a statement that's you:

Traditional

AT HOME

Anne and Jeffrey Smith
1 Main Street
Roseville, CA 00000
876-555-9865
aandjsmith@anywebsite.com

Nontraditional

After the honeymoon, you can reach us at:

1 Main Street
Roseville, CA 00000
876-555-9865
aandjsmith@anywebsite.com
Anne and Jeff Smith

Nontraditional

Keep in Touch!
We'd love to hear from you ☺
Anne and Jeff Smith
1 Main Street
Roseville, CA 00000
876-555-9865
aandjsmith@anywebsite.com

Ordering Professionally Made At-Home Cards

You may see the option to order professionally made At-Home cards together in a matching set when you buy your invitations, inserts and thank-you-note cards. Everything is made from the same card stock, with matching fonts, in your choice of color, engraved, thermographed or letterpressed as you've selected for your invitations. The At-Home cards then are yours to design in your chosen professional style, and they'll be part of the shipment on that exciting day when your invitations show up. If that date has passed already, and you only now have your new At-Home residence and phone to share, you can *still* go back to your source and order professionally printed At-Home cards to send with your thank-you notes. For a professional job, you'll follow all the same planning and ordering rules as in chapter 19, checking the same resources plus others you may discover in the meantime. You might order in a stationery store, through an order form presented by your wedding coordinator (and ask your florist, who usually has options for you as well!), or online. Just as with professionally printed *anythings*, be sure you've carefully checked that all of your information is correct—it would be a shame to get one digit wrong in your phone number—and that the numbers and letters are all legible as written in your chosen font.

Making Your Own

If you'd rather not order professionally made At-Home cards but would prefer to make your own, again, follow the details in chapter 20. Use your printer's or copier's fine-print setting rather than normal settings for the best result, and check out glossy papers and vellums. Your printer should have a setting to accept either of these options, and you should use that great straight-line paper cutter for a clean finish on the edges. You'll find the perfect cards for this task in the office supply or craft store, looking in the stationery section for packs of note cards, postcards or even oversized place cards in pretty colors, with borders, or with graphics to match your thank-you notes' stock. You can embellish this card as you wish, with a monogram sticker, decorative sticker, rubber stamp marking, or other accent. You can also hole-punch the card for a bit of added flair, such as with a tiny heart cutout in the corner, or a more intricate Cupid, butterfly or any number of creative hole-punch options. This cutout could match the one on your thank-you note, or it could be reserved just for this special little card alone, to set it apart. Be sure the color of print matches that of your thank-you note, or is in a complementary color that works well with your chosen color theme for this mailing. For instance, your thank-you note print could be a mix of hunter and sage greens, and your At-Home card features hunter green print only. Or, you'll use a darker rose color for your At-Home card for an eye-catching kick within the green print of your thank-you note. It's your creation, and since you're the artist, you get to play with several color combinations while trying out prints on plain sheets of paper (before using your card stock for the real copies).

CHAPTER 25

Stylish Extras

These days, many brides and grooms are also choosing to add "a little something extra" in their thank-you notes. It may be a great photo as mentioned earlier, or a beautiful poem or quote printed up on a translucent piece of vellum. (For sample quotes, check out pages 211–216 in the Appendix.) If you didn't have room on your thank-you note, if an additional quote or lengthy poem would have made your card too "busy" or cluttered, this insert gives you the perfect place to add your chosen expression.

For example, imagine a light lavender piece of vellum fluttering out of your thank-you note as the recipient opens it. In lovely italic print, the saying is:

"What lies behind us and what lies before us
are tiny matters compared to
what lies within us."

— RALPH WALDO EMERSON

or

"Life is either a daring adventure
or nothing at all."

— HELEN KELLER

Your thank-you note, then, becomes an opportunity for you to share a gem of wisdom as well. And you never know who among your guests could use a dose of wisdom at the time.

Wisdom and inspiring sayings, your favorite Bible scripture or psalm or bits of humor are popular choices for these stylish extras — whatever you might wish to come fluttering out of your thank-you note and bring a smile to the face of your recipient.

Other options to consider include:

- **A postcard with a great, inspiring or funny saying on it, postage stamped by you for their use**. They can then reach out to someone in their lives with a hello, a thank you or an invitation to connect over coffee. It's a "Pay It Forward" kind of thing that you put in motion.

- **A bookmark with a terrific quote on it.** Check at your favorite chain or independent bookstore to find amazing and artistic bookmarks in either laminated card stock, stitched leather, fabric with a silver charm or shaped metal stamped with a quote. Other sources for terrific bookmarks: museum stores and online sites, art fairs where you can make the day of an artist or work-at-home par-

What *Not* to Enclose . . .

This is a thank-you note, not a business networking tool. So keep the business cards, your company brochure, your profile in the company newsletter, your fund-raising requests, your kids' fund-raising requests and any other business items out of the envelope. Couples who have crossed the line between gratitude and self-promotion have raised some eyebrows and burned some bridges. Your thank-you notes should elicit smiles, not a sour taste in the mouth. Don't blindside your guests with an advertisement of any kind.

ent by snapping up all one hundred of her creations, and Native American craft shops. Bookmarks may even be made on your home computer using graphics software, your own digital picture (perhaps that great shot of a butterfly or rainbow you took on your honeymoon) and glossy bookmark paper stock.

- **Card deck entries.** Those boxed card decks featuring a different saying on each beautiful card are perfect as stylish extras. Just buy two or three decks, and use each card individually as inserts in your thank-you notes. You'll share inspiration, or some Zen advice, a relaxation tip, a great date idea or any other topic you choose with each of your guests.

- **Laminated pocket cards from the stationery store.** You may find the perfect wallet-sized add-in for your thank-you note. A *"Start with Dessert First!"* card, for instance, could remind your guests to savor the sweet things in life.

- **A magnet.** Perfect for the refrigerator as a daily reminder, magnets are the new hot insert of choice. (Granted, you'll have to write a note on the envelope that a magnet is enclosed, due to the damage that could happen if that magnet gets anywhere near an important computer disk on your recipient's desk.) Check your craft or office supply stores for the products to make your own, or see the sites listed in the Resource section for more ideas.

- **A copy of your own artwork,** such as a watercolor of pink calla lilies or beachscape, printed on glossy paper and ready for framing.

- **A print of a graphic you love,** such as a close-up of a bright orange gerbera daisy that you've either photographed yourself or found online. Again, use the glossy photo paper from an office supply store.

- **A good-luck charm,** such as a four-leaf clover or a fortune symbol print. You're just sharing your prosperity with others.

PART SIX

Thank-You Gifts

You may wish to say thank you with a gift as well as with a note. Your wedding coordinator may have been such a doll that you wish to send flowers. Your parents may have outdone themselves with their generosity, so you're searching for the perfect gift for them. And that bridesmaid who saved the day? She certainly deserves a present for her generosity of spirit. Now all you have to do is find the perfect thing.

In this section, you'll find a range of suggestions for wrapped gifts, gift certificates, and guest hotel room welcome baskets that will pamper and impress those who came all this way to be with you.

CHAPTER 26

Gift Ideas for Special People

As an added thank you, sometimes a gift is in order. You may have already planned out your gratitude gifts to your bridal party—perhaps wedding-day necklaces for the ladies and tie clasps for the men—as well as special gifts of thanks for your parents, such as tickets to a concert or dinner at their favorite five-star restaurant. These wonderful people in your inner circle have been there for you, and you may not have been able to plan the wedding of your dreams without them. Whether they've written checks or whipped out their credit cards to get you everything from your gown to your bouquet to the amazing reception you've always wanted, planned your shower or flew in for your big day, these nearest and dearest have come through for you.

At the end of this chapter, I've listed some top choices in thank-you gifts. You'll also find some terrific websites in the Resource section for you to check out. But first, as a reminder, consider as gift recipients the following people who *also* did so much to make your wedding dreams come true:

- **The parents of the child attendants.** They shopped for those cute little dresses, got you a gift, devoted their time to bringing the children to fittings or parties and to the wedding itself. In our time-crunched world, this kind of dedication should be thanked with more than just a card.

- **Those outside the bridal party who helped you with the plans.** Sure, they said it's their pleasure to help make the favors, or bake one hundred cupcakes, but their generosity of spirit warrants a token of your gratitude.

- **Those who shared their contacts with you.** Without Cousin Lucy's recommendation of your cake baker, you wouldn't have had that amazing five-tiered masterpiece at a "friend's discount." Cousin Lucy made it possible. Think back over all the helpful people who suggested great experts, sites, places to take your pictures and Web resources to check out.

- **Your wedding experts . . . and their assistants.** Especially the assistants, if you worked with or through them often. These essential helpers are often the key to the final results you enjoy, so make their day (or year) by thanking them with a little something special.

- **People who allow your wedding guests or bridal party members (and their dates, sometimes!) to stay at their houses rather than getting a hotel room.** Their gift of hospitality to others makes it possible for those others to give the gift of their presence to you! So reward them nicely with a little something to show you appreciate it.

- **Your travel agent.** Again, it's her job to set you up with a great honeymoon, or those group tickets for your destination wedding, but it's wonderful when you stop in after the honeymoon to drop off a basket of flowers or a box of chocolates. Plus, her boss will take notice of your appreciation and effort in thanking her.

- **The valet parkers, coat check staff and other helpers on the big day.** They may live for tips, but what a great thing for you to end your wedding celebration by handing them each a small gift as well as a smile, a hug and an in-person thank you. One coat check attendant told me, "I couldn't believe they thought of giving me a box of chocolates! I always feel invisible to the wedding guests and especially the bride and groom." Your thoughtful gesture could mean more to a worker than you can imagine.

Take Your Pick!

For any recipient, you can choose from an enormous range of gifts. Inexpensive items like boxes of pretty note cards or boxes of truffles are an easy purchase, and loftier picks like monogrammed cashmere blankets for those "above and beyond" folks are worth the investment for the joy they bring.

Here are some ideas to get you started, and I encourage you to check out some of the terrific specialty gift websites (in the Resources section) where you can enter your price range and gift theme to reveal the top, trendiest selections.

Bouquets of flowers	Bookstore gift cards
Bottles of wine	Boxed note card sets
Gourmet sauce sets	Coffee baskets
Picnic baskets	Martini sets
Spa robes	Photo albums
Candles and holders	Watches
Tickets to a game	Flasks

Gifts for Kids

What do you buy the child or teen who has everything? Go age-appropriate, and get parents' input. You may find out about a much-wished-for toy or collectible, a sports hero whose autograph you can get while you're at the game, a handheld game or the new, hot games for an existing gadget, jewelry, music CDs, a popular children's book that's just been released, tickets to a concert *the parents agree to first*, gift cards to a favorite clothing store, gift cards for teen spa treatments and décor for their rooms.

Coffee table books

Potted flowers

Bottles of champagne

Cheese board sets with slicers

Picnic blankets with monograms

Spa pampering kits

Garden stones

Tickets to a show

Dinner gift cards

Aromatherapy sets

Vases for flowers

Ice cream sets, cups and spoons

Charm bracelets

Cufflinks

Colognes and perfumes

Art books

Potted plants or herbs

Olive oil sets

Marble coasters

Cashmere throws

Music CD sets

Wind chimes

Spa gift cards

Journals

Tea sets, with cups

Sushi sets

Bookends

Initial necklaces

Travel kits

Lip gloss kits

Cookbooks (a big trend!)

And of course, there's always the much-appreciated silver picture frame, in a range of styles. Family photos, after all, are cherished possessions in the home or office, so you can't lose with a sleek and sophisticated silver frame featuring a laser-cut design, intricate accents or a truly unique style.

CHAPTER 27

Guest Hotel Room Gift Baskets

Thank your guests upon their arrival for your wedding weekend by giving them a gift basket filled with terrific snacks or pampering products. They've come a long way to be with you, and even though you've planned a terrific weekend for them (including your wedding), it's a fabulous gesture of thanks to give them a collection of treats for during their stay. The bag or basket of goodies will be waiting for them in their room or handed to them at the front desk with a big smile and welcome. Or, if guests will be staying at a private home, you'll drop them off ahead of time, perhaps setting them on a bedside table. "Thanks for being here, and the fun begins now!" is the message of the welcome gift basket.

Lately, this tradition has grown from a "nice little something" that a smattering of brides and grooms chose to arrange into almost a "must." So many couples are creating gift bags that it's become something of a com-

Who Gets a Basket?

Don't make the number-one guest gift basket mistake: giving to some, but not others. Full-scale grudges have evolved out of such perceived "favoritism," so be sure to give the same baskets to all of the following:

- **Guests staying at *any* hotel for your wedding weekend.** If you've given them choices of nearby hotels, perhaps offering a range of budget fits, you'll give the same basket to those in the cheaper hotel as in the expensive one.

- **Guests staying at friends' and family members' houses nearby.** Just because they're not staying in the hotel doesn't mean they don't deserve a welcome basket, too.

- **Guests staying at your house.**

- **Bridal party members who are staying with friends.** Yes, you've already gotten them bridal party gifts, but this extra welcome basket is a wonderful offering on your part.

- **Children and teens.** They should get their own separate, customized baskets (more on what to give kids later in this chapter).

- **One for the groom if he's not staying with you the night before the wedding.** His welcome basket can contain his favorite snacks and soft drinks, perhaps a bottle of wine, a special gift from you, a card from you and a napkin imprinted with a lipstick kiss from you.

petition, like the Oscars swag bags without the keys to a Vespa or a $150,000 watch. You don't have to be extravagant with these gift bags or baskets—no season tickets to a sports team or complimentary weekend at an Arizona spa needed. It's the little things that make all the difference: a box of chocolates, bottled water, comfy socks. These three are actually among the most appreciated gifts mentioned by wedding guests. Here are some of the top items usually included in guest welcome gift baskets (and in a moment, I'll share with you the new, hot items to add):

- Comfy socks

- Bottles of water

- Cans or bottles of soda

- Chocolates

- Candies and candy bars

- Crackers

- Packets of cookies like Oreos or Mrs. Fields

- Homemade chocolate chip cookies, bagged

- Gum and mints

- Breakfast bars or energy bars

- Pampering items like a small bottle of lotion or aromatherapy body oils

The new, hot items now being added to the basket are:

- Gift certificates for brand-name coffee houses like Starbucks or Dunkin' Donuts (as in, "Coffee's on us all weekend!")

- Bottles of coffee drinks

- Cans of flavored iced tea drinks

- Herbal tea packets with bagged cookies or tea bread slices, biscotti or lemon pound cake

- Room scent spritzers in travel-size bottles (lavender is a top choice, with eucalyptus, spearmint, vanilla, and tropical flower scents also in the favorites category)

- Massage oils and instructional books or cards on how to give a great massage or foot massage

- Pedicure kits, with toe dividers, nail polish colors and foot creams

- Copies of regional magazines, featuring listings of what's going on around town, restaurant and martini bar ads and flagged pages featuring items of interest to the guest (such as children's activities, seasonal festivals, golf courses, tennis courts . . . personalized to each guest)

- Printouts of the local movie theater schedule

- Car air fresheners, to make their ride to the wedding smell sweet

- Gift books, such as little collections of love quotes or poetry, and inspirational or quirky card decks found at the bookstore

- Prepaid phone cards, so that guests can call their kids back home without having to use their own minutes

Romantic Gift Baskets

An always-welcome theme in the welcome gift basket realm is giving items to make the guests' weekend extra-romantic. That means massage oils and lotions, music CDs, chocolate-covered strawberries or truffles they can feed one another, bubble bath or fabulous bath additions like rose petal–shaped scented drop-ins for the tub, even a bag of actual rose petals to sprinkle on the bed or the floor leading up to the bed. Include blank cards the guests can use to write each other love notes, or pink heart-shaped Post-it notes they can use to leave one another love notes on the bathroom mirror. Add a fun pen from the party supply store, such as one with heart shapes on it, or a fluffy feather top. Think of the little things you both bring home when you want a romantic night in, and inspire your guests to skip that movie at the cineplex in favor of a nice night spent in the room, giving and receiving massages. They'll soon be saying, "Thank *You!*"

Keep It Clean!

Of course, you know that fuzzy handcuffs and sex toys are on the market, and you may know that your friends would *love* the edible whipped body cream. But I must advise you to keep your choices more romantic than X-rated, as you don't want to offend some of your guests who may not share your open mind about that sort of thing.

Gourmet Gift Baskets

Keep your guests out of the minibar by adding some gourmet treats to the mix. While everyone loves their favorites, Kit Kat bars and Oreos for instance, think about taking a walk through some great stores for unique gourmet treats instead. Give guests a bite of something unexpected, like jalapeno sourdough pretzels, wasabi peas, blackberry and currant jam for those crackers, fresh bread or rolls and a mini bottle of olive oil with dipping plates in the basket.

My favorite sources for great guest room gourmet gift baskets are wine and cheese stores, where you'll find amazing packaged snacks such as Asiago cheese crackers, even chocolate truffles made with various wines, pretzels in unexpected flavors like mesquite and ranch, flatbreads and crackers, caramel popcorn with a kick and of course, crowd-pleasers like cashews and macadamia nuts. Look past those amazing vintages to the snack aisle and gourmet munchie section for inspiration.

The health food store is also a great place to pick up unique snacks, always nonrefrigerated things that can be kept in the room without having to put on ice. Here, you'll find healthy snack bars, cups of nuts and granola, veggie chips and salsa, even turkey jerky that I'm told is a big hit in welcome baskets.

For cookies and biscotti, chocolate-covered fruits and coffee cakes, breads and Italian breadsticks, hit the bakery section of your supermarket or your favorite bakery in town. You'll also find jars of tapenade and olives, as well as rosemary oils and gourmet vinegars.

You have so many options when it comes to gourmet gift baskets and may even discover new favorite treats of your own. Or, if you're feeling industrious, your gourmet gift basket can be entirely self-made, and if you bake, you can share your famous oatmeal cookies, homemade chocolates, banana nut bread or trail mix. This personal touch can make all the difference with a welcome thank you that's truly from the heart.

Pampering Basket

Think of the kinds of pampering products you like to receive as gifts, the ones that relax your shoulders down to where they should be and make you feel blissful. Your welcome basket could give your guests an instant mood lift as the ultimate in thanks. Think of relaxing aromatherapy products like lavender and vanilla, eucalyptus and sandalwood, jasmine and ocean breeze scents. Or energize your guests with a citrus scent. Look at hand and foot creams, body lotions, oils, nail creams, lip balms, avocado butter hair masques, honey foot scrubs. Check out those pre-packaged pampering kits at gift shops and stores like Target and Bed Bath & Beyond. You'll find white tea collections, green tea collections, hibiscus, rose scent and vanilla, already put together in handy zip cases your guests can use as travel pouches later.

And don't forget the men! They love their pampering products as well, so look for men's lotions, soaps and creams in pre-packaged collections at Target or Wal-Mart, at the men's counter in a department store, or at beauty supply shops that stock these kits for men.

Take the well-being basket up a level with a great music CD. In our stressful times, it's hard to unwind (it's hard to *remember* to unwind), so your "welcome and thank you for coming" gift basket could remind them that it's okay to let go of work and travel stress for the weekend of your wedding. You've given them the tools to do so, and all you want for them is to relax and enjoy their time away from home.

On the Wedding Day Basket

You're just happy your guests are here, and you want to make the wedding day even better for them. So fill their welcome basket with items they'll need on the big day, like sunscreen and mosquito-repellant wipes (choose a natural or organic product), fun sunglasses for an outdoor wedding, a one-time use camera (brilliant to give it to them now, so that they can use it throughout the weekend, giving you both much better pictures than they would take just at the reception!), gum and mints for fresh breath and a fresh copy of directions to both the ceremony and reception sites. You might even include an itinerary of all the wedding weekend events you have planned, with contact cell phone numbers and driving directions for the ultimate thinking-of-you basket collection. Your guests will appreciate the time you took to arrange everything they'll need.

Kids' Baskets

Kids will very likely bring their own handheld game systems, so you won't need to set them up with activity-type items. Rather, create a basket with snacks they'll love, mixing up some healthier choices with the expected candies and cookies. Children's books are a very popular trend for this basket, especially if you can find a tie-in to popular kids' cartoon characters or movie heroes. Check the bookstore for kids' character tie-in items like sticker books and games, music CDs they can listen to in the car, even lunchboxes or carry bags that you can use *as* their basket.

Make your choices age-appropriate, and if you're not sure of what fits a five-year-old as opposed to a ten-year-old, ask the children's parents for ideas. Not everything has to be a surprise, so it's wise to get parents' input . . . especially if you'll be putting food items into the kids' bags. Parents may have strict rules about snacks, and kids may have allergies. So ask for some ideas to give yourself the best chance of creating a successful kids' basket.

Teens should get their own separate baskets, filled with age-appropriate items like snacks and bottles of water or iced tea, sodas, gum, a pre-paid phone card for that all-important call back home to a boyfriend or girlfriend, a magazine and a gift card for a nearby shop like a music store or sporting goods store, an accessories shop or a bookstore.

Basket or Bag?

It's your choice whether to use a great woven or iron basket or a decorated gift bag that's big enough to hold your welcome gifts. It's only a matter of finding the perfect color or style that works with the theme of your collection. You might choose, for instance, an apple-red gift bag filled with goodies and orange tissue paper on top for a festive look. Or a white bag with pink tissue paper. You might choose Mexican-style woven baskets with a great design, or a chic hot-pink clear plastic case that zips at the top in a perfect use-again style.

Check party supply stores, craft stores, even dollar stores and card stores for a great selection of containers. Or visit websites that sell unique bags and boxes that will suit your "thank you for coming" packages in unexpected ways. Your guests will marvel at the container before even opening it.

Spa Visits

The big thing in guest welcome gift baskets is a gift certificate for a manicure or pampering treatment at the hotel's on-site spa. Great for teens and adult guests, you're sharing the royal treatment with them. You can ask the hotel manager for discounts on group purchases of gift cards for your guests, and will likely receive a nice percentage off. Your guests of all ages will be *thrilled* to find these thank-you cards in their welcome baskets.

And of Course, a Thank-You Note . . .

Within your gift baskets, always attach or include a personalized note from the two of you, thanking your guests for coming to your wedding:

Dear Jim and Eliza:

> *Thank you so much for coming to our wedding! We're so glad you've arrived safely and we can't wait to celebrate with you! In the meantime, we hope you enjoy these treats!*

> *See you soon!*
> *Matt and Adrienne*

Welcome to New York City!

You've arrived, baby! It means so much to us that you're here for the wedding, and while we wish we could welcome you in person, we're running around like maniacs right now! So enjoy these little gifts until we can give you a big hug in person—

Renata and Kyle

Thank you so much for traveling all this way to be with us!
After such a long flight, we thought you could use a little pampering. So sit back, relax and enjoy these goodies . . .

We can't wait to see you!
Lila and Dennis

A NOTE FROM THE AUTHOR

Now that you have a plan for writing out all of your many, diverse thank-you notes all the way through your own personal "wedding season," you can look forward to the process. Rather than dread the work ahead, take a few moments before you lift your pen and think about how lucky you are to have so many people to thank! Don't confuse your blessings and your burdens—the size of your thank-you note to-do list is a direct reflection on just how much kindness and generosity you've received since Minute One. How lucky you are to have so many wonderful people in your life!

Take your time, don't rush and break the job down into several sessions . . . to keep your mind fresh and your hands from cramping! This is a job you both can share, and you'll reflect on the joy of your pre-wedding and wedding day moments with each envelope you seal.

I applaud you for your generosity of spirit! The fact that you invested in this book shows that you consider it a priority to thank your loved ones well; not just properly, but from the heart. They too are lucky to have *you*, and I know that your gracious notes will be well-received.

—Sharon Naylor

APPENDIX

Here you'll find the useful tools that will allow you to create your thank-you notes with style, and with easy organization:

- Your Thank-You-Note Thesaurus, to help you select the perfect phrasing and eliminate the monotony of writing the same thing over and over and over again

- Quotes About Gratitude, to share a classic or contemporary quote that captures the sentiment just right, as an accent to your note or as a printed enclosure for the recipient's display

- Thank-You Checklists

- Do-It-Yourself Shopping List

- Writing Timetable

- Resources

Your Thank-You-Note Thesaurus

Check out the following synonyms for the most common thank-you-note vocabulary, looking of course for words you would actually use in real-life conversation. If you feel some synonyms are a bit flowery or formal, just look for the ones that fit your style best.

Thrilled: captivated, celebrating, charmed, delighted, ecstatic, elated, enchanted, enraptured, entranced, euphoric, excited, fulfilled, glad, gladdened, gratified, joyous, overjoyed, pleased, rejoicing, tickled

Perfect: absolute, accomplished, beyond compare, classic, consummate, crowning, excellent, expert, faultless, finished, flawless, ideal, immaculate, impeccable, masterful, masterly, matchless, peerless, pure, skilled, skillful, sound, splendid, sublime, superb, supreme, unequaled

Gratitude: appreciation, grace, gratefulness, honor, indebtedness, obligation, praise, recognition, thankfulness, thanks, thanksgiving

Appreciation: admiration, appraisal, assessment, attraction, commendation, comprehension, enjoyment, esteem, high regard, love, perception, realization, recognition, regard, relish, respect, sensibility, sensitiveness, sensitivity, understanding

Beautiful: admirable, adorable, alluring, angelic, appealing, beauteous, bewitching, captivating, charming, classy, comely, cute, dazzling, delicate, delightful, divine, elegant, enchanting, engaging, enticing, enthralling, excellent, exquisite, fair, fascinating, fetching, fine, glamorous, good-looking, gorgeous, graceful, grand, handsome, ideal, lovely, magnificent, marvelous, nice, pleasing, pretty, radiant, ravishing, refined, resplendent, splendid, stunning, sublime, superb, well-formed, winning, wonderful

Gift: contribution, courtesy, endowment, fairing, favor, goodie, largesse, legacy, offering, present, presentation, provision, token, tribute

Talent (as in, "You have such a talent for finding the perfect gift!"): ability, accomplishment, acquirement, adeptness, adroitness, aptitude, aptness, attribute, bent, capability, capacity, cleverness, command, competence, craft, endowment, expertise, faculty, finesse, flair, forte, deftness, genius, handiness, ingenuity, instinct, knack, know-how, leaning, mastery, power, proficiency, propensity, resourcefulness, savvy, skill, specialty

Generosity: altruism, amity, benevolence, compassion, feeling, friendliness, friendship, gift, goodness, goodwill, humanity, kindheartedness, kindness

Considerate: accommodating, amiable, attentive, benevolent, big, charitable, chivalrous, circumspect, compassionate, complaisant, concerned, cool, discreet, generous, kind, kindly, magnanimous, mindful, obliging, polite, tactful, tender, thoughtful, unselfish, warmhearted

Very: absolutely, acutely, amply, astonishingly, awfully, certainly, considerably, dearly, decidedly, deeply, eminently, emphatically, exceedingly, excessively, extensively, extraordinarily, extremely, greatly, highly, incredibly, indispensably, largely, notably, noticeably, particularly, positively, powerfully, pressingly, pretty, prodigiously, profoundly, really, remarkably, substantially, superlatively, surpassingly, surprisingly, terribly, truly, uncommonly, unusually, vastly, wonderfully

Openers and Closers

You may also wish to add some variety to the openings and closings of your thank-you notes . . . here are some twists you can take on the tried-and-true. The opener usually doesn't command as much attention as the rest of what you write, so you'll be fine if you choose to go with the straight "Dear Mary," too!

Hello Mary!

So great to see you again, Mary!

Greetings from the returned newlyweds!

We're home!

We're back!

To our favorite host,

To our dearest friend,

Dearest Mary,

As for your closing phrases, you might wish to sign off with *Love, (your names)*. However, you don't have to sign every card *Love*, especially when notes are given to bosses, colleagues, friends and family you've never used the L-word with. Alternatives you might consider include:

Love always,

All our love,

With our thanks and love,

With our gratitude for your generosity and love,

With all best wishes,

All the best,

We love you!

With our best wishes for *(fill in the blank)*

Warmly,

Warm regards,

Warmest regards,

Warmest wishes,

Blessings, *(this is the new popular choice, showing up more and more!)*

Cheers!

Aloha *(especially if headed off to a Hawaiian honeymoon or if the wedding was held in Hawaii)*

Gracias,

Big hugs to you!

Hugs and kisses to you all!

The following phrases are considered a bit more formal, and have fallen out of favor:

Fondly,

Affectionately,

Best,

Cordially,

Quotes About Gratitude

"We can only be said to be alive in those moments when our hearts are conscious of our treasures."

— THORNTON WILDER

"The smallest act of kindness is worth more than the grandest intention."

— OSCAR WILDE

"I awoke this morning with devout thanksgiving for my friends, the old and the new."

—RALPH WALDO EMERSON

"At times our own light goes out and is rekindled by a spark from another person. Each of us has cause to think with deep gratitude of those who have lighted the flame within us."

—ALBERT SCHWEITZER

"Appreciation can make a day, even change a life. Your willingness to put it into words is all that is necessary."

—MARGARET COUSINS

"When you have once seen the glow of happiness on the face of a beloved person, you know that a man can have no vocation but to awaken that light on the faces surrounding him; and you are torn by the thought of the unhappiness and night you cast, by the mere fact of living, in the hearts you encounter."

—ALBERT CAMUS

"There is not a more pleasing exercise of the mind than gratitude. It is accompanied with such an inward satisfaction that the duty is sufficiently rewarded by the performance."

—JOSEPH ADDISON

"As we express our gratitude, we must never forget that the highest appreciation is not to utter words, but to live by them."

—JOHN FITZGERALD KENNEDY

"Feeling gratitude and not expressing it is like wrapping a present and not giving it."

—WILLIAM ARTHUR WARD

"You give but little when you give of your possessions. It is when you give of yourself that you truly give."

—KAHLIL GIBRAN, *THE PROPHET*

"God's gifts put man's best dreams to shame."

—ELIZABETH BARRETT BROWNING

"How far that little candle throws his beams
So shines a good deed in a weary world."

—WILLIAM SHAKESPEARE

"Remember God's bounty in the year. String the pearls of His favor. Hide the dark parts, except so far as they are breaking out in light! Give this one day to thanks, to joy, to gratitude!"

—HENRY WARD BEECHER

"I am a part of all that I have met."

—Alfred Lord Tennyson

"We cannot live for ourselves alone. Our lives are connected by a thousand invisible threads, and along these sympathetic fibers, our actions run as causes and return to us as results."

—Herman Melville

"If the only prayer you said in your whole life was, 'thank you,' that would suffice."

—Meister Eckhart

"If you have lived, take thankfully the past."

—John Dryden

"For each new morning with its light,
For rest and shelter of the night,
For health and food, for love and friends,
For everything Thy goodness sends."

—Ralph Waldo Emerson

"The unthankful heart . . . discovers no mercies; but let the thankful heart sweep through the day and, as the magnet finds the iron, so it will find, in every hour, some heavenly blessings!"

—Henry Ward Beecher

"Who does not thank for little will not thank for much."

— ESTONIAN PROVERB

"There is nothing like a dream to create the future."

— VICTOR HUGO

"There is no beautifier of complexion, or form, or behavior, like the wish to scatter joy and not pain around us. 'Tis good to give a stranger a meal, or a night's lodging. 'Tis better to be hospitable to his good meaning and thought, and give courage to a companion. We must be as courteous to a man as we are to a picture, which we are willing to give the advantage of a good light."

— RALPH WALDO EMERSON

"We make a living by what we get, but we make a life by what we give."

— WINSTON CHURCHILL

"No one has ever become poor by giving."

— ANNE FRANK

"A thing of beauty is a joy forever."

— JOHN KEATS

"Gratitude is the memory of the heart."

—JEAN BAPTISTE MASSIEU

"Silent gratitude isn't much use to anyone."

—G. B. STERN

Thank-You Checklists

Engagement Party

Name	Thank-You Note Sent (✔)
_____	_____
_____	_____
_____	_____
_____	_____
_____	_____
_____	_____
_____	_____
_____	_____
_____	_____
_____	_____

Name	Thank-You Note Sent (✔)

Shower #1

Name

*Thank-You Note
Sent (✔)*

_____ _____

_____ _____

_____ _____

_____ _____

_____ _____

_____ _____

_____ _____

_____ _____

_____ _____

_____ _____

_____ _____

_____ _____

_____ _____

_____ _____

_____ _____

_____ _____

	Thank-You Note
Name	*Sent (✔)*
_____	_____
_____	_____
_____	_____
_____	_____
_____	_____
_____	_____
_____	_____
_____	_____
_____	_____
_____	_____
_____	_____
_____	_____
_____	_____
_____	_____
_____	_____
_____	_____
_____	_____
_____	_____
_____	_____
_____	_____

Shower #2

Name	Thank-You Note Sent (✔)
_____	_____
_____	_____
_____	_____
_____	_____
_____	_____
_____	_____
_____	_____
_____	_____
_____	_____
_____	_____
_____	_____
_____	_____
_____	_____
_____	_____
_____	_____
_____	_____
_____	_____

Name	Thank-You Note Sent (✔)
_____	_____
_____	_____
_____	_____
_____	_____
_____	_____
_____	_____
_____	_____
_____	_____
_____	_____
_____	_____
_____	_____
_____	_____
_____	_____
_____	_____
_____	_____
_____	_____
_____	_____
_____	_____
_____	_____
_____	_____
_____	_____

Parents, Bridal Party Members, Grandparents and Others

Name	Thank-You Note Sent (✔)
_____	_____
_____	_____
_____	_____
_____	_____
_____	_____
_____	_____
_____	_____
_____	_____
_____	_____
_____	_____
_____	_____
_____	_____
_____	_____
_____	_____
_____	_____

Name

Thank-You Note
Sent (✔)

_____ _____

_____ _____

_____ _____

_____ _____

_____ _____

_____ _____

_____ _____

_____ _____

_____ _____

_____ _____

_____ _____

_____ _____

_____ _____

_____ _____

_____ _____

_____ _____

_____ _____

_____ _____

_____ _____

Wedding Gifts

Name	Thank-You Note Sent (✔)
_____	_____
_____	_____
_____	_____
_____	_____
_____	_____
_____	_____
_____	_____
_____	_____
_____	_____
_____	_____
_____	_____
_____	_____
_____	_____
_____	_____
_____	_____
_____	_____

Name	Thank-You Note Sent (✔)
_____	_____
_____	_____
_____	_____
_____	_____
_____	_____
_____	_____
_____	_____
_____	_____
_____	_____
_____	_____
_____	_____
_____	_____
_____	_____
_____	_____
_____	_____
_____	_____
_____	_____
_____	_____
_____	_____

Wedding Experts

Name	Thank-You Note Sent (✔)
_____	_____
_____	_____
_____	_____
_____	_____
_____	_____
_____	_____
_____	_____
_____	_____
_____	_____
_____	_____
_____	_____
_____	_____
_____	_____
_____	_____
_____	_____
_____	_____
_____	_____

Name

*Thank-You Note
Sent (✔)*

_____   _____

_____   _____

_____   _____

_____   _____

_____   _____

_____   _____

_____   _____

_____   _____

_____   _____

_____   _____

_____   _____

_____   _____

_____   _____

_____   _____

_____   _____

_____   _____

_____   _____

_____   _____

_____   _____

Additional Thank Yous

Name	Reason	Thank-You Note Sent (✔)
_____	_____	_____
_____	_____	_____
_____	_____	_____
_____	_____	_____
_____	_____	_____
_____	_____	_____
_____	_____	_____
_____	_____	_____
_____	_____	_____
_____	_____	_____
_____	_____	_____
_____	_____	_____
_____	_____	_____
_____	_____	_____
_____	_____	_____
_____	_____	_____
_____	_____	_____

Name	Reason	*Thank-You Note* Sent (✔)
_____	_____	_____
_____	_____	_____
_____	_____	_____
_____	_____	_____
_____	_____	_____
_____	_____	_____
_____	_____	_____
_____	_____	_____
_____	_____	_____
_____	_____	_____
_____	_____	_____
_____	_____	_____
_____	_____	_____
_____	_____	_____
_____	_____	_____
_____	_____	_____

Do-It-Yourself Shopping List

___ Thank-you note cards or papers

___ Envelopes

___ Vellum overlays

___ Insert cards

___ Ink cartridges, black

___ Ink cartridges, color

___ Invitation software

___ Stamps and ink pads

___ Embossing supplies

___ Monogram stickers

___ Decorative or theme stickers

___ Hole punches, standard or shaped

___ Scissors, standard or border-shaped-edged

___ Ribbon

___ Wax seal sets

___ Postage stamps

___ Copies of graphics or wedding portraits

___ Gel pens

___ Calligraphy pens

___ Calligraphy pen sets

___ Scrapbooking cutouts

___ Stick-on borders

___ Additional inserts _____

_____

Your Writing Timetable

Schedule your writing sessions here, and mark them in your calendar or BlackBerry as an appointment the two of you have with one another for this important and timely task.

Date   *Time*   *Place*

_____   _____   _____

_____   _____   _____

_____   _____   _____

_____   _____   _____

_____   _____   _____

_____   _____   _____

_____   _____   _____

_____   _____   _____

_____   _____   _____

_____   _____   _____

_____   _____   _____

Resources

Office Supply Stores

www.officedepot.com

www.officemax.com

www.staples.com

Papers and Card Stock

All of the above, plus the following specialty sites:

http://paper.com

www.artpaper.com

www.botanicalpaperworks.com

www.flaxart.com

www.hqpapermaker.com

www.legionpaper.com

www.mcgpaper.com

www.redrivercatalog.com

For specialty gift boxes and gift bags,
check out www.bayleysboxes.com

Scrapbooking Sites

www.exposuresonline.com

www.michaels.com

www.scrapjazz.com

Craft Sites

www.flaxart.com

www.michaels.com

Also, see the listing for office supply stores.

Labels

www.amazinglabels.com

www.colorfulimages.com

www.familylabels.com

www.friendlyfacesonline.com

www.labelcreations.com

www.vistaprint.com

Software

www.mountaincow.com
(Look for Printing Press Platinum, a program you can use
for thank yous, wedding weekend invitations, as well as for
all future parties and celebrations you will have.)

E-mail Greeting Websites

www.123greetings.com

www.bluemountainarts.com

www.hallmark.com

Gift Websites

www.berries.com (chocolate-covered strawberries)

www.blisstrips.com (relaxing music and guided meditation CDs)

www.cherylandcompany.com

www.exposuresonline.com

www.giftbagboutique.com

www.godiva.com

www.letme.com

www.mms.com (This is the official site for M&Ms brand candies, where you can *personalize* the colors and a message on M&Ms!)

www.oprah.com (Boutique sales support her Angel Network)

www.pajamagram.com

www.presentpicker.com

www.target.com

www.walmart.com

www.yankeecandle.com

INDEX

Page numbers in *italic* indicate figures; those in **bold** indicate tables.